How True

How True

A SKEPTIC'S GUIDE TO BELIEVING THE NEWS

by
THOMAS GRIFFITH

An Atlantic Monthly Press Book
Little, Brown and Company • Boston • Toronto

FIRST EDITION
T04/74

A portion of this book appeared
in *The Atlantic*.

Library of Congress Cataloging in Publication Data

Griffith, Thomas.
How true: a skeptic's guide to believing the news.

"An Atlantic Monthly Press book."
1. Journalism—United States. 2. Journalists—
Correspondence, reminiscences, etc. I. Title.
PN4867.G7   070.4'0973   73-22488
ISBN 0-316-32867-7

ATLANTIC—LITTLE, BROWN BOOKS
ARE PUBLISHED BY
LITTLE, BROWN AND COMPANY
IN ASSOCIATION WITH
THE ATLANTIC MONTHLY PRESS

Published simultaneously in Canada
by Little, Brown & Company (Canada) Limited

PRINTED IN THE UNITED STATES OF AMERICA

To the memory of my sister Catherine

". . . *neither ought any thing to seem to be spoken truly, because eloquently; nor therefore falsely because the utterance of the lips is inharmonious; nor, again, therefore true, because rudely delivered; nor therefore false, because the language is rich; but that wisdom and folly, are as wholesome and unwholesome food; and adorned or unadorned phrases, as courtly or country vessels; either kinds of meat may be served up in either kind of dishes.*"

— *St. Augustine,* The Confessions

"*The truth just doesn't lie somewhere in between. It's wherever it is.*"

— *James R. Hoffa*

CONTENTS

How True

1

TRUTH

Who wants the truth and nothing but the truth? A steady diet of truth would sear the stomach lining; falsity is essential to our well-being, and permeates our lives.

Businessmen tell the hard truths about their doings only to the extent required by law. Governments lie. Politicians dissemble. Trial lawyers, when they can't challenge the facts, plant doubts. Whole industries live on pretense, by flattering your self-importance in exchange for your money, by rearranging reality. The stewardess's smile, the salesman's heartiness, the test kitchen's unnatural neatness, the headwaiter's solicitude, the athlete — after the mayhem stops — giving locker-room interviews full of modesty and benevolence, the doctor's tempered reassurances, the desperate stratagems of aging actresses. The false fronts of buildings, and the false fronts of self: girdles, hair coloring, suntans.

There is also the falsity that is kindness: comfort given to

3

buck up others, wounding truths unspoken; feelings concealed, spared or feigned. The useful falsity of office mateyness, exchanges without genuine feeling; the borrowed sentiments of greeting cards.

There is the falsity that is self-indulgence, since most people want no clear-cut verdicts on themselves, and devise social strategies to avoid them. When reality is too unbearable, they drink to avoid it, travel to escape it, fantasize to deny it. Friendship is often a mutually agreed upon assurance, sometimes against the evidence, of the meaning and importance of each other's lives. Whole industries exist to provide solace, appearances, illusions. One must be able to eat the steak without thinking of the abattoir. Even in small matters people resist reality: they take pictures to remember how something was, but first tidy up the room, and neaten their clothes. They want newspapers to print the truth, but as concerns themselves, only that part of the truth that puts them in a favorable light.

Into all this comes the journalist, demanding on behalf of others to know the truth and to disseminate it.

2

APPEARANCES

It is a strange feeling to spend years working at a craft, convinced that you know what is generally right and wrong about it, only to discover that many people — possibly most — feel differently than you do about it, dispute your pride in it, and question its values.

Perhaps this may in recent years be a common experience in many fields, since so much has come under severe scrutiny, whether it be the practice of law or medicine, the role of the church, the responsibility of business. That scrutiny for a time promised to be revolutionary, and had about it some of the heedless, headlong quality of revolutions: unknown leaders raising new flags and shouting accusations; their followers self-righteous, impatient, idealistic, scornful. A revolution, ill-defined but broad, seemed to be sweeping all before it as it assaulted the citadels of power, and for a time the center wavered, but then held. That revolution cannot be said to have won, since it did not come to power; neither can it be said to have lost, since those in power prevailed only by promising to be more amenable to change, and sometimes becoming so.

The disarray in my own field, which is journalism, was doubly marked, for not only was it charged with recording these stormings of the citadel and all the sideline guerrilla skirmishes, but was itself a confused participant in the action. It took me a while to recognize journalism's role as participant, because of a lifetime's contented belief in its being outside, and perhaps above, the battle.[1]

A journalist's valuable, inescapable and contentious task is to tell his fellow citizens what is going on in their times. Those of us who were drawn to our craft believing it an exciting way to do good must now concede that our self-esteem seems not entirely to be shared by the public. In popular judgment (or so we are assured) to be a journalist is to be a man slightly suspect, a perverter of truth, an invader of privacy, a disturber of the peace, a sensationalist, a simplifier.

The pollster Louis Harris, who regularly measures how public opinion ranks various occupations, finds journalists scoring considerably below doctors, bankers, congressmen, the military, teachers, preachers, and business executives in public confidence. What is more disquieting about Harris's figures is that, until Watergate at least temporarily halted the decline, the esteem in which journalists are held had

[1] As much as possible the word media will be avoided in this book. I remember an occasion when my late boss Henry R. Luce was badgering Winston Churchill, wanting to know why in office Churchill was less eager to join Europe than he had been when out of power. Evidently joining Europe was one more diminution of the British Empire that Churchill was unwilling to preside over. He growled at Luce: "I will not be dealt with as part of a blob!" Neither will I. The ugly word media should be left to advertising men, who regard newspapers, radio, television and magazines indifferently as media in which to peddle their wares. Journalism, a word of honorable lineage, includes radio and television when I speak of it. We're all in this together.

dropped 11 percent since 1966 — during a time when, by the old craft standards by which the press measures how well it does its job, it was probably performing better than ever before in circumstances considerably more difficult.

Most journalists I know are bewildered by the evidence that their calling is more lowly regarded than it once was. They thought they had outlived that irresponsible era when, as a nineteenth-century etiquette book advised the well-bred, it was improper to order a newspaperman kicked down the stairs since he was merely making his living in a disagreeable way. Journalists are no longer the hard-boiled, hard-drinking cynics of *Front Page* days; they are college-educated and purposeful, they think themselves responsible professionals and can be humorlessly priggish about the salty, legendary old days. They, so energetically exposing the misdeeds of others, shining the clear white lamp of truth into the darkened corners of corruption, are they *themselves* mistrusted? Yes.

The trouble isn't just that the press is unfairly denounced by opportunistic politicians, though there is plenty of that. Nor is it enough to say — as many journalists do, with a trace of self-righteousness — that no one likes the bearer of bad tidings. The difficulty has to do with who can be believed these days. That has always been a preoccupation of journalists, but now the question is properly directed at themselves.

Is the mistrust greater because journalists are more visible? I think so. There they are, the flower of the Washington press corps, scrambling at White House press conferences (when there are any), seeking the President's attention, asking questions that are often pertinent, sometimes personal, occasionally pompous, frequently rambling. And if you are a supporter of the President's, the questions may strike you as rude and his reticences quite proper. In fact,

7

unless you are incorrigibly hostile to a President of the United States, you must hope that he will prove in command of his subject and have nothing to hide: that this lone Daniel will be able to quiet the assembled pawing and snarling lions.

I wince for my craft even more when I watch that familiar televised scene outside a courthouse, where an emerging witness is gang assaulted by agile and rude reporters, out-elbowing one another to thrust a mike into someone's face, calling out brazen questions while the camera moves in close to study the witness's demeanor. Innocent or guilty, that witness had some protection inside the courtroom in the rules of evidence and the presumption of innocence. Here in the street he is jostled, barbarically accused, and watched and judged by whether he stammers, evades or panics — a rough justice that is as final and more arbitrary than a jury's verdict. This is the modern equivalent of putting people in the stocks in the public square — except that in colonial days someone had first to be declared guilty.

Are they all, in this baying pack, even journalists? Who is to tell? There are no admittance cards to this scrimmage; anyone can jostle or throw a loaded question, and we now know that after the inquest at Chappaquiddick, the roughest innuendoes disguised as questions came from a bogus journalist from the Nixon "dirty tricks" squad. But even when all questioners are bona fide reporters, there exists a difference between print and electronic journalists. It would be ungallant to suggest that of the two a newspaperman is invariably more experienced or better mannered. Perhaps the distinction is that a newspaperman usually wants more elaboration on a specific point, while a television reporter wants to elicit on camera a dramatic reaction from the witness, and for this purpose the ruder, the more personal, the more outrageous the question, the better.

In the guise of bringing you real-life reporting, the camera is in fact skipping one of the essential, protective steps in the reportorial process. A print reporter, trying to encompass all the possible ramifications of a story, will ask searching and awkward questions, but if the answer to them is no and he has no reason to challenge that response, he leaves such an unconfirmed suspicion out of his story. In the televised street gathering, the same question lingers in the air as an accusation, and stays in the audience's mind. Television thus involves its audience in its complicity. It brings you a visual reality which you yourself witness and believe to be true, for to think otherwise would be to doubt your own eyes and ears. And it makes *you* the judge in cases where you have heard little of the evidence and can only see the behavior of the witness reacting under stress. Those familiar sidewalk kangaroo trials give journalism a bad name, but I deplore them more for the injustice they do.

Should I acknowledge a bias? Any pencil journalist envies the television intruder whose open-lensed stare gives a clearer picture of what the journalist can only describe; television can reach its audience before the reporter even gets back to the office to write up his story; and its bulky presence transforms an occasion, making any witness self-conscious and more guarded in his responses.

So often what television shows you may be "true" as a photograph, while false in what it suggests. Usually television cameras can only stand outside a door, or witness posed cordialities before a door closes (Presidents and visiting heads of state become practiced at this ritual, which gives no clue to the character of the actual meeting). Television can't often show you the trial, the hearing or the cabinet meeting, or give you many of the details about them, which it leaves to other reporters to gather laboriously; its stage-lit interviews of officials are frequently a free ride on those newsmen whose digging has brought the camera to the scene; its street corner interviews a burlesque of opinion sampling, random and misleading; its foreshortening of all but the most major events has the same relationship to reality as do television's commercials showing floors swiftly waxed or a headache's quick relief.

Television's deficiencies thus add force to the widespread dissatisfaction with journalism, but they are not the real source of the discontent, which goes deeper. All of us journalists who have chronicled the disorder of our times have lately been brought up short by the realization that to large segments of the public we are not regarded as neutral carriers of this report, but are included in the skepticism and animosity, and suffer similarly a decline in authority. It is necessary to think anew of what journalists do and what can rightfully be expected of them. That will be the jousting ground of this book.

My theme is how journalism affects the times it sets out to record. My account will be personal, because I believe journalism to be inevitably subjective. I cannot promise you dangerous exploits, for though my work has taken me around the world, I usually get to work by crosstown bus. When I am autobiographical I mean only to show how attitudes form and choices are made. I don't seek to persuade you to my own reading of events so much as to show you how I was influenced by them, or had to guard against them. My narrative is only a clothesline on which to hang my views. My intention is to examine the mysterious, unacknowledged (and at times, unconsidered) reasons why the press behaves as it does. Some of what it does, it shouldn't do; but often what it does, though unpopular, it must do. The confusion between these two aspects of its performance is what I propose to explore. I do not think it possible to rest content with the pat defenses that journalism offers to its critics.

To begin with, journalism is not a profession. It lacks that first essential of a profession, rules for admission. Hairdressers even have that. Wrongdoers in journalism, instead of being censured, are more often highly rewarded, for in journalism the theatrical often prevails over the reliable.

Journalists sometimes think of themselves as members of a priesthood, though they have never agreed on a set of vows. Still, all honor to that priestly impulse, which accounts for much of the best in journalism. But it would be nearer reality to think of journalists as an inner clan within a wider tribe; in practice, journalism includes not only the work of professionals but of others who have only visiting privileges as journalists, and must reckon with their imagination and knowledge as well as in some cases with the swagger and distortion of their personalities. Ah, but that isn't journalism, some professionals will say: that's show business. I grant that the inclusion of these outsiders makes it harder, though not impossible, to talk of journalistic standards. But it is journalism's own proprietors who have given these people, on the air or in print, the status of journalists.

Ours is a profession only in the interior aspirations and accomplishments of those who are dedicated to it — men who wouldn't want to do, or be, anything else. It is run from the countinghouse. Somewhere in the background can usually be heard the ring of the cash register, or else the clang of an alarm bell over the cash register's silence.

Journalists are thus in a position quite common in American life, of feeling loyalties toward a craft which may at times run counter to the needs or advantages of its owners. In this respect we are like technicians in drug laboratories or design engineers in automobile plants: our skills are necessary and frequently well-rewarded; certain craft protections as well as better pay have been slowly won by the efforts of persistent men; and honorable people on both sides have worked out strategies and nuances to preserve honesty and independence. My asperity about owners doesn't suggest that any alternative form of ownership, including the Marxist, would be preferable. But to many — and perhaps most — of the owners and corporate managers of television stations, newspapers and magazines, journalistic principles are apt to be considered a mystery, a handicap or an expense. To them, journalism of the conventional kind (the kind that the high priests of journalism most frequently dogmatize about) does not draw well enough or sell well enough.

But who then adds the adulterant? Was it at the sales force's insistence, or was it the Detroit design engineers in their eagerness for salable novelty, who gave automobiles their tail fins? In journalism the competitive instinct among reporters and editors themselves creates not only an incentive to outperform but also the drive to outsell. The rivalry among what are now four competing brands of journalism — newspapers, magazines, radio and television — who compete not only for audiences but also for advertisers, has led to an increased sophistication in whoring after audiences.

The impact of such pandering, and the distortion it produces, is best studied at those ramshackle rites of democracy, the political conventions. These gatherings are such farces in themselves, and are so overlaid by the forces of attendant journalism, that the reality (if there is one) becomes invisible in the glare. Convention halls are no longer even laid out for the benefit of delegates who are presumably assembled there to deliberate. In the choicest spot in the center of the hall rises a mounted platform, as sacred and massive as the great Caaba of Mecca, for cameramen to focus on the speaker's podium; around this vast mount, which effectively blocks the view behind it, the rows of state delegations are laid out. Delegates themselves seem less the hearty hypocrites of old, the crude, dealing politicians, but more respectable types who have been coached in how to dress and how to behave under the roving eye of restless cameramen looking for cameos of real-life boredom, of delegates or onlookers yawning, talking, fidgeting while overhead the loudspeakers roar out the oratory that is unlistened to except at climactic moments in the hall, and is perhaps not even broadcast to the rest of the nation.

For the most familiar convention television shot of all is that of one of the network's lofty news-stars, sitting high in his glass booth at one end of the hall, looking disapprovingly down at the droning speaker on the platform below and turning back to find his next commercial message or a few words by himself, or some minor commotion back at a candidate's headquarters, more engrossing than the convention proceedings. In this he may be right. At least, in the competition between networks, it is their own busywork, and not the convention itself, which holds an audience to CBS or NBC or ABC.

To catch a television producer's eye, which is the first step in catching the public's eye, convention programmers have shortened their sessions, changed their hours, and recruited their platform speakers from Hollywood, from major league locker rooms and from outer space. Still the camera's attention wanders. Reformers have suggested that public television at least should keep its camera on the convention podium. The question is not whether such a program would be endurable, but whether it would reflect the actuality of a convention any better.

Now add in some other star turns and sideshows. One network stages a daily slanging match at the scene between representatives of left and right (Buckley vs. Vidal or Galbraith) whose coyly wicked exchanges proceed from assumed philosophical differences that have been reduced to stylized prop gags like Jack Benny's violin. Newspapers and magazines too no longer depend on conventional coverage and hire such impressionistic observers as Norman Mailer, Gloria Steinem, Wilfred Sheed and Renata Adler, who report the gaudy doings with their own skewed perceptiveness.[2] Then come the satirists, Russell Baker and Art Buchwald, converting the outlandish into the absurd. When even so self-respecting a newspaper as the New York *Times* has sent to the scene, besides its platoons of reporters and columnists, a humorist, a society party watcher and its restaurant sampling expert, how is *Esquire* going to top that act? By importing three writers whom no one can possibly accuse of a serious interest in American politics — William (*Naked Lunch*) Burroughs, poet Allan Ginsberg and the avant-garde French playwright Jean Genet.

At what point in this melancholy declension did such coverage cease to be journalism? It was not the convention's press credentials committee that bestowed the status of journalist on all the specialists and all the freaks. The journalistic industries legitimized them. In this way coverage overwhelmed the event, and condescended to it.

How then is it any longer possible to think of journalists (as I once did) as white-coated technicians, living in a germ-free space capsule, looking out detachedly at the wrangling universe? How is it possible to define, let alone defend, such a motley? The task becomes more like defending law or medicine: how many fatigued and devoted physicians must be placed on the scale against malpractitioners or high income quacks to give medicine a good name; how many

---

[2] Mailer was *Life*'s 1972 convention choice when I was its editor.

scrupulous and forbearing lawyers to offset the shysters and the show-offs?

But there *is* a central core of practice to examine. It would offend fairness to attack all journalism for the misdeeds of the worst, just as it would offend truth to cite only the best as a way to defend the rest.

3

BIAS

Nothing irritates a journalist so much as to be told that he is
biased, particularly when the charge comes from someone so
blinded by his own prejudices that he wouldn't know evenhandedness if it smote him on both cheeks evenhandedly.
The journalist is usually goaded into insisting that he isn't
at all biased, an innocent state of mind impossible to prove.
Better to admit from the start the inevitable subjectivity of
journalism, and then to treat it as a necessary condition, not
a right.

On the newspaper where I once worked, an only-the-facts-
ma'am style of writing prevailed. In the areas we were allowed to report about, we were confined to the barren facts;
the result was that the most conscientious reader hardly
knew what was really going on in the city. Later I went to
work for *Time* magazine. In its original prospectus, written
twenty years earlier, two impish young men fresh out of

Yale had proclaimed the impossibility of objectivity. They confessed to certain biases, such as a conviction that the world was round and the cost of government rising too fast; they acknowledged a preference for the new, particularly in ideas, and a respect for the old, particularly in manners. These were engaging and undemanding admissions, but the principle itself was invoked in later years for some quite outrageous distortion of the news, which took *Time* years to live down. The assertion of nonobjectivity made possible the opinionated compression of the newsmagazines, which have proved a surprisingly durable form for fifty years. Slow to allow such bold appraisals of events in their news columns, newspapers still fastidiously label them "interpretation" or "analysis," as if everything else they printed had been subjected neither to analysis nor to interpretation.

Quite intelligent people can sometimes be heard saying that all they want from the press is the facts; they'll make up their own minds. T. S. Eliot once urged poets to "let the facts generalize themselves" but such advice is less helpful to journalists. Of course, "facts" such as stock market closings and batting averages can and do pass into print without comment, and traffic accidents can be reported "straight." If that were all journalism is about! Much else, and that which matters most, requires selection and judgment. Think of all that is said aloud every day the world over — of those Arab parliaments echoing with vituperation (which is the second leading export of Arab nations, after oil) of the stately nonsense and occasional late afternoon eloquence in the House of Commons, the windy indulgences that fill column after column of the *Congressional Record,* and then the jabber of a thousand city councils, school boards, library committees. All those egos! You can question a journalist's choice, but not his need to choose.

Not that selecting what is quotable out of the daily din of

overstatement and contrived outrage is all that difficult. Most newsmen, confronted by a text, leap to the same passages. The best quotes may even have been pointed out in advance by a politician's press aide, for the canniest of politicians exist in their quotability.[1]

That news is such an agreed quality — that deskmen at news agencies and in a thousand city rooms make up their minds so swiftly, and react in much the same way to the worth of a news story and the length it should be — says much about training and professional habits, but says more about the routineness of what passes for news. Practiced, no-nonsense deskmen know how to scourge copy of emotive words, at which point an editor is apt to congratulate himself on the objectivity of what he has wrought. When that mood steals over him is when he should be most on guard. An unaware bias, or a bias denied, is the worst kind. It suggests lack of imagination, and usually goes with the kind of journalism that isn't doing enough to serve its readers. That kind of look-no-hands objectivity has never quite recovered from Senator Joseph McCarthy, who taught journalists a hard lesson in responsibility. It wasn't enough to quote neutrally McCarthy's every lie and libel, reassuring oneself that "he said it, didn't he?" and "we can always print a later denial," for this was to give demagoguery a head start. As Mark Twain said, a lie can travel halfway around the world while the truth is putting on its shoes.

No, the real question of bias begins earlier, in what is pursued, or not pursued, as news. A news story originates in a collision of fact with an interested mind, and what makes

[1] Spiro Agnew and his speech writers, for example, worked hardest on those bombastic phrases in his speech that they knew would make the kleig lights turn on to record a minute's snippet for the evening television news. More qualified passages, suggesting that Agnew knew better, were buried in muted portions of his speech. And then, with the hypocrisy and gall that comes so easily in public life, Agnew would sometimes argue that the "media" had played up only his more tendentious remarks.

one journalist "see" a story and another not has much to do with his own imagination, curiosity and temperament. Other craftsmen, the copy editors, can later deprive the writer's words of any hint of feeling (such scrubbing is not very demanding work), so that an article reads as if the reporter were as impersonally fashioned of metal as his typewriter. But the reader who thinks that the news can be delivered untouched by human hands and uncorrupted by human minds is living in a state of vincible ignorance.

Some news "happens," the rest is discerned. And it is this process of discovery of the news that is most mysterious, and most creative. Journalism is not an inexact science; it is not a science at all. Nonetheless, there are certain parallels to the scientific method.

In England in recent years a considerable debate has gone on about just how science makes its discoveries, and the argument is quite relevant to the journalistic practice of finding news. As Sir Peter Medawar, the biologist, has described the situation in *The Listener,* English science was for a long time under the spell of John Stuart Mill and his notions of inductive reasoning. The job of science was to observe nature objectively (it was assumed that objectivity was possible) and then to put these facts into sensible order. From this wrong conception of the scientist's role, Medawar thinks, came "the tragedy of the two cultures . . . the entirely erroneous belief that there is an enormous gap between people like artists and poets and writers, who work through the imagination, and scientists, who are, intellectually speaking, rude mechanicals."

The man who refined the scientific method, and who in Medawar's belief will survive in history as a greater philosopher of science than Francis Bacon, is Sir Karl Popper, a Viennese intellectual who migrated to England after the

Second World War. In *The Logic of Scientific Discovery,* Popper challenges the notion of science as mere objective observation. Instead, he believes that all the basic discoveries of science originate in a hypothesis — an imaginative preconception of what the truth might be. (Ernst Cassirer once put it another way: "Experience presupposes an intellectual 'sketch' of the thought, Galileo's *mente concipio,* with which we anticipate a regularity in nature; we raise the sketch to certainty by testing it through experience.")

The scientific hypothesis determines what is to be observed, and what is not to be. It should forecast what future observations or experiments will show, and must be put in such a way as to be tested, or, as Popper calls it, *falsified* by systematic attempts to refute it. In this testing, or second step of the scientific process, objectivity is not only possible but essential. If experiments go against the theory it is, of course, disproved; if they confirm the forecasts, the theory is still not said to have been proved, only to have passed a test successfully.

In a sense, science is a history of superseded theories, some of which, like Newton's theory of gravitation, have a long run before being regarded as untenable. To Hermann Bondi, a theoretical astronomer at the University of London, and another admirer of Popper's, a scientific theory is alive only as it lives dangerously, and must go on making further forecasts of what future evidence will show. "In science," Bondi declared over the BBC, "it isn't a question of who is right and who is wrong: it is much more a question of who is useful, who is stimulating, who has helped things forward. I like scientists who are quite passionate about their ideas. But they must always realize that the value of their ideas lies in how disprovable they are, in what tests they attract and in what discussions they stimulate."

It is easy to see how scientists find such an approach congenial to them. It gives imagination a central place in their work and dignifies the dogged corroboratory process as a step in further development, not merely as an attempt to shoot down a colleague's theory. The parallel to journalism of Popper's scientific method is one that a journalist must draw modestly, for the testing of his own ideas before he commits them to print can never be called scientific. Yet the process that Popper describes — of conjecture subject to verification — has much in common with how a journalist's mind works. He has a notion of something that needs looking into, usually in a gap he has spotted between what a situation is generally understood to be, or what someone claims it to be, and what he thinks inquiry will show. He senses a disparity between promise and performance, reads some figures that don't stand up, gets a tip from some dissenter within the ranks, and sets to work.

Now the second stage of Popper's process takes over. Now it becomes necessary to comprehend all the essential elements of a situation, to seek explanations from all who are involved, to check out the discrepancies between one person's version and another's, until the reality comes clearer. This is the cooler, more relentless process of verification. The most brilliant of journalists, those whose ideas are more audacious and invaluable, sometimes lack the stamina for patient detailed investigation, or are reluctant to surrender an idea that didn't prove out; it is left to the more methodical members of the press to follow through. They may be eager to knock down a competitor's story, may lack some of the final neutrality of the laboratory, but this too adds something to the rigor with which assertions are tested.

Journalism even more than science is subject to Heisenberg's effect — the recognition that what is observed may be affected by the fact of observation. Once a pack of journalists goes baying after a scent, the pursuit takes on a momentum of its own; pressure builds up on those who have been silent or who have something to conceal; they may no longer be able to ride it out. Others, often out of partisan promptings, join in and keep the subject alive; grand juries or legislative committees elicit in sworn testimony answers that might have been refused a mere nosy journalist. Such a progression was most evident in the Watergate affair; the White House dismissal of it as a "third-rate burglary attempt" might have prevailed but for the persevering efforts of two Washington *Post* reporters, working with leaks from those in government who thought the truth shouldn't be hidden. Yet only when the law itself, an impatient federal judge and an aroused Senate, invoked their powers of subpoena, of grand jury testimony and of televised hearings under oath, did the full story begin to come clear.

In the end, issues of misfeasance or malfeasance are determined by the courts; if not, the final decision will come from the "court of public opinion," before which journalists as much as anyone else must plead their cases. That court is not bound by the rules of evidence, nor by the objective standards of the scientific laboratory. Courts of public opinion hand down three kinds of verdicts: guilty, not guilty or not interested.

To me, to be professional is not to be without bias (the self is always present in the seeing) but to be self-aware. There are newsmen who believe they should be untouched by what they see; not me. I know of no newsman at Dallas whose emotions weren't torn loose by President Kennedy's assassination; but with however big a lump in their throats they got the word over the air, or steadied themselves down to gather all the facts for the stories they wrote. A big moment, even a tragic one, thrills a journalist, or he would be in some other line of work: it supplies the adrenalin he needs to get the story fast and tell it well. Suspect an indifference that calls itself impartiality; it is the pedestrian asset of second-raters.

Nor can ideas be judged by journalists who are without ideas of their own. Every good journalist I know has convictions; he also has a combative sense of right and wrong, and a shrewd intuition about which people in public life embody one or the other. Critics, discovering the presence of such attitudes in newsmen — and it is evident enough in their after-hours conversation — find this discovery proof conclusive that the journalist has his thumb on the scale. But a good journalist is an unreliable ally to any cause he believes in, as his friends in public life soon learn. His refusal to wear campaign buttons or to applaud speeches is but an outward demonstration of his belief that to enlist in any cause may be to prejudice his coverage. And it is in this capacity to separate his beliefs from his reporting that a journalist should be judged. Spiro Agnew thought it enough to label journalists as liberals in order to establish their untrustworthiness, which is the method of a smearer in all ages. In the 1972 campaign the Nixon people had gathered all the sticks of evidence they could find to show the bias of the liberal press, but never got the chance to light their fire. For along came Thomas Eagleton's concealed psychiatric treatment and George McGovern's disingenuous handling of it; reporters went in hot pursuit of the story, though it would result in the discrediting of their presumed favorite, Senator McGovern. That episode ensured the Nixon landslide, but never produced an acknowledgment by the Nixon administration that the press can be trusted to forget its prejudices when a story cries for telling.

The true relationship between a journalist's beliefs and his reporting is something like that of a juror's desire to reach an impartial verdict. Jurors are not required to be empty minds, free of past experience or views; what is properly demanded of them is a readiness to put prejudices and uncorroborated impressions aside in considering the evidence before them. As much is asked of the journalist.

Journalists who once spoke of their objectivity now generally accept fairness as the criterion of their performance. This suggests that subjectivity is natural, and fairness a reasoned control of one's bias. The best of contemporary journalism meets this test, but I am not sure that in doing so the problem is fully resolved.

To me, bias is more elemental. It is really about sympathy given or sympathy withheld, and is so pervasive in everyone (we all "make allowances" for conduct in friends that we should deplore in others) that it is hard to root out. Journalists are not surgeons and our scalpels are not sterilized; we ourselves can be infected. In my own case, I find it difficult to write understandingly about the banal, the brutal, the greedy and the craven: hard to sympathize with people who have everything and are discontent; hardest of all to give sympathy to those who give no sympathy to others. "To understand all is to pardon all" is a resonant French sentiment, but I don't share it. I think that I understand a lot that I don't pardon. These are prejudices of mine that exist at a level deeper than political partisanship, which one learns to compensate for.

Journalists are not eunuchs; they have views and sympathies; they are saved, when they are saved, by their skepticism and by their need not merely to theorize but to ground themselves in the particular. A similar alert skepticism is required of any reader if he would judge what out of all that wears the name of journalism is to be trusted or discounted, for the final step in the making of public opinion is the active discrimination of those who are audience.

Once a reader or listener asks himself whether he prefers columnists or commentators because their views are similar to his own, once he tests what he reads or listens to not by whether it dares to have a point of view but by whether that point of view properly reckons in all that might be said against its thesis, he may find himself revising his notion of what in journalism is most deserving of trust. And reading alertly and skeptically in this way, he might discover another impediment to getting the facts straight. For at this point he would be beginning the fascinating exploration of his own biases.

4

Memory Cell: SEATTLE

Of late a modish kind of journalism has called itself new. People speak of the new journalism, or of advocacy journalism, and though the two forms differ, they share a common distaste for flat and factual reporting. New journalists have about them a strong streak of show biz, and a frank admiration for the techniques of fiction. They write well, though sometimes excessively. They live at the intersection of fact and fiction, so that the reader is not sure whether the subject confided his thoughts to the writer, or the writer imagined the quotes. The most talented of them, Tom Wolfe, who wrote a notoriously fictional profile of *The New Yorker*'s editor filled with telling details which proved not to be so, has described the process:

The passion of the new nonfiction is . . . a matter not of projecting your emotions into the story but of getting inside the emotions, inside the subjective reality of the people you are writing about. I often enter into a kind of controlled trance — that's the only way I can think of describing it — when I am writing a scene. What I am trying to do is relive somebody else's emotional experience in my mind.

The new journalism also encourages heart-on-the-sleeve involvement, such as this passage from an article in *New York* magazine: "Let me confess to you up front that for me this article has been a rotten personal trip. It took me nine wretched weeks to write, ending up with three hours of hysterical tears." I find it hard to continue reading such an article with confidence.

New journalism as a valid personal kind of writing, using the techniques of fiction but adhering to the discipline of facts, is better observed in Norman Mailer, whom I once signed up to cover the landing on the moon for *Life*. Our magazine owned exclusive rights to the astronauts' own stories, an arrangement designed by the astronauts' lawyer so that their families would not be pestered by mobs of reporters, and would share equally in the considerable profits. I always felt *Life*'s contract a dubious idea; since taxpayers were investing billions in the space program, the story belonged in the public domain, and *Life*'s exclusivity was properly resented by the rest of the press. Inevitably the astronauts began telling their experiences fully at televised press conferences after each moonshot, leaving little fresh to be said in the following week's *Life*. So *Life* turned to stories about the astronauts' wives, though there was always something macabre about photographing and describing their reactions to blast-offs that might end tragically for their husbands, a situation that was saved only by the tact and sympathy of such *Life* writers as Loudon Wainwright and Dodie Hamblin. As the novelty of the wives' tales wore off too, *Life* sent a science fiction writer, Ray Bradbury, to cover one launch, and the poet James Dickey to another.

One night, at one of those bizarre advertising-promotional dinners where celebrities of all descriptions intermingle (among the honored guests was the girl whose expansive bosom had stopped traffic in Wall Street) I was seated between Norman Mailer and Deke Slayton, the boss of the astronauts. Midway in the dinner Janis Joplin, the rock singer, approached our table, disheveled hair hiding her face from us. Her sullen accompanist trailed her. Our table seemed much too sedate for her, so she began spraying us all with four-letter words. Marge Slayton, the astronaut's wife, being both relaxed and generous, found Janis Joplin's conduct not so much unforgivable as unnecessary. Mailer leaned over to assure her in a patronizing way that four-letter words were merely the harmless direct honesty of the young. I found myself saying "Oh come off it, Mailer. Everybody speaks several languages, according to the occasion. You may have spoken army at Harvard — but I'll bet you didn't speak Harvard in the army."

He didn't react as pugnaciously as I had expected, for as I later came to know, Mailer is a canny mixture of outrage and control. The evening ended well; Joplin returned to our table to pat Marge Slayton's head in shy apology, and the Slaytons and I ended a snowy night at Mailer's Brooklyn Heights home overlooking the Manhattan harbor. From the pleasure of that evening came the notion to match Mailer and the moonshot, but I soon discovered that Mailer comes high; he had nineteen people to support — parents, ex-wives, children — and his agent told me that conversation starts at four hundred thousand dollars, with a book in it at the end. And so began for me the discovery of a writer who scorned the conventions of journalism but who at his best was one of the best journalists around.

For *Life,* Mailer went on to cover prizefights and political conventions. He brought the reader the Mailer version of any occasion, but was meticulous in his quoting, and far from going into a trance or tears before covering a story, went into training like a boxer, giving up whiskey so that his senses would be alert, prowled endlessly about, gathering impressionistic details of the raunchy and scruffy motel and military-industrial side of Cape Canaveral as well as admiring the test-pilot professionalism of the astronauts.[1] His observing eye and his inner eye are both hard at work — seeing the scene and at the same moment interviewing his own reactions to it. I liked in him an audacity in risk taking that I lacked in myself, whether it meant inviting dangerous physical experience or the extended reach of his metaphors. Though his is show-biz journalism and chancier for being that, I thought he added a dimension of observer-and-observed to journalism, as did some of our own writers on *Life,* Joan Didion, Wainwright, Tommy Thompson, Barry Farrell, Joan Barthel, Shana Alexander and others.

Such punctiliousness, of labeling speculation as such, and insistence on carefully researched fact, to me was the essential distinction between this kind of participatory journalism and the winging-it, interior trance school which argues that if it seems that way to me, who needs facts? (Mailer's worst is in that category.)

Tom Wolfe's conception of journalism reminds me more of the "March of Time" radio days in the 1930s, when an actor who could brilliantly mimic Franklin Roosevelt's voice

---

[1] Slayton and most of the other astronauts, however, were leery of what Mailer might say about them, and *Life* was never able to get Mailer the access to the astronauts that our other writers had. Mailer's own reaction to this suspicion was that, while he might savage any of his fellow writers, he would never put down those who, like Indianapolis race drivers or astronauts, were doing what he couldn't. He finally concluded that he would prefer anyway to write about the astronauts at a distance, without incurring any obligations to them.

would describe how FDR "really" felt about men and issues. When the White House protested, Henry Luce defended the practice with Calvinist conviction. Those made-up quotes in FDR's voice, Luce was to plead, were "fakery in allegiance to the truth." Wolfe and Luce are welcome to that line of argument.

Advocacy journalists, the other branch of the new journalism, are not fictionalists but polemicists. They believe all journalism bloodless that isn't pushing a thesis, are never content to describe or explain a situation but get in front of the reader pointing out who are the black hats and who the white hats, tediously moralizing and making their own virtues and bravery perfectly evident. These new partisans are often lively, their causes worthy (though not always), their passion commendable. Yet finally, advocacy is destructive of what journalism is all about, to the degree that it feels no need to scruple about accuracy, to get the whole story or to give the other side its due. I cannot conceive of a world, even a brave new world, that doesn't depend on all the facts being known, and not just the convenient ones.

Besides, I've been there before. Journalism that felt little duty to be fair to all sides, and free to push a thesis and to conceal facts awkward to it, was the prevailing style on most American newspapers when I entered the business in the depression year of 1936, newly graduated from college. Of course, distinction must be drawn between writers and editors subject, as we were in those days, to the dictates of willful and authoritarian publishers, and the indulgent laxity of the new journalism which perverts the truth in the name of heightened drama. The difference between these two situations is fundamental if you are a writer. It is less so if you are a reader, for the end result in either case is journalism that is not to be fully trusted.

As a journalism student at the University of Washington I had filled my head with ideals, had learned a little about the practice of journalism, and had scorned the local newspapers in Seattle for their mediocrity and their betrayals. With the diploma put away in the drawer, I was grateful to go to work at twenty-five dollars a week for the richest and most conservative local paper. At least it wasn't working for Hearst, whose heavy paw lay all over the morning paper.

The Seattle *Times* was the personal fief of an autocratic old character named General Blethen, whose swift rise in National Guard rank took place far from any battlefield and depended more on his capacity to help or hinder a succession of Republican governors. The General was portly but did have a presence, a harrumphing parade-ground authority. His displeasure on whatever trivial grounds could be absolute. Sam Groff, one of our best reporters, had earlier been a cartoonist on the rival and feeble Seattle *Star,* where he had frequently caricatured the General as a tiny fellow overwhelmed by his uniform, with epaulets as big as street brooms, and a sword trailing the ground behind him on a roller skate wheel. One day, shortly after joining the *Times,* Sam was summoned to the General's office; sure that his cartooning past had caught up with him, Sam went expecting to be fired. Instead the General with unsuspected shyness asked whether he might have one of Sam's old caricatures to keep.

Sam's fears were simple prudence in those depression days when one clung desperately to jobs. We were warned that anyone who referred in print to *shipping* instead of *sending* a body back home could expect to visit the cashier for his final paycheck. The severe competition from radio led to this passage in our paper's stylebook: "Once a reporter wrote a feature yarn full of sob stuff about a little boy who found his dog after making an appeal by radio. A few days later the reporter found that the radio stations had nothing more to offer him than the newspapers."

We were hired help, all right. A few years later the Blethens, who thought themselves stern, paternalistic and generous — and who did in fact pay salaries that were marginally better than the city's two chain newspapers — found themselves with a union in their city room. It arrived painfully, sundering the common esprit of the city room, opposed by most of the senior plantation hands and supported with misgivings by the rest of us. In addition to following the crotchets of the General, which we were habituated to, would we now be told by union leaders what to write?

The General's crotchets were, of course, royal writ to us. Society hostesses who had offended the Blethens were not to be named in print (a practice that is familiar enough in American journalism). Democrats were mentioned only for their transgressions, while the dullest utterances of Republicans made page one. And then there were our "campaigns." These weren't as idiosyncratic as on the morning Hearst paper. Hearst filled his columns with obligatory nonsense about antivivisection, the red menace and the yellow peril; these were interspersed with scandals told with pious hypocrisy, exposing sinners caught in "love nests," at a time when Hearst himself and his mistress Marion Davies were eating off the gold plates at San Simeon. Our own campaigns were sometimes silly, and sometimes serious, but in either case had to be solemnly waged. Day after day, our front page stories denounced a proposed highway through a park (gas fumes would kill the animals in the zoo, our paper warned) when the General's primary objection was that another route would have been more favorable to his real estate holdings.

We worked in the smog of his whims. As police reporter, if the fire department ticker indicated an alarm came from a box anywhere near our building, I was to drop everything, find out about it, and report to the city desk before the General called to ask where the engines were headed. From his habit of following fire engines from his office window, or looking down on fender-bender traffic accidents in Times Square, came the practice of putting a Big Window mark on any piece of copy involving the General's enthusiasms or taboos. This cabalistic device was, I believe, unknown to him.[2]

So intense was our paper's antagonism to labor, in the strongly unionized city of Seattle, that no Big Window was needed to make sure that our bias was a manifest in print. The first day I went to work for the *Times,* a front page editorial in blackest Gothic ended: HOW DO YOU LIKE THE LOOK OF DAVE BECK'S GUN? THE SHAME OF IT!

The General's choice of target was correct and courageous. Teamsters were taking over the city, encouraged by Franklin D. Roosevelt's new labor laws; their ambition was to organize "everything on wheels" and if successful could shut down the entire city if they wanted to. They already could prevent rolls of newsprint from reaching our plant, or printed papers from leaving it, so the General's attack on the teamsters took nerve. The union's goon squads roamed the city, unchallenged by the police, dumping dye in the vats of dry cleaners whose plants were not unionized, or beating up teamster members who at meetings had dared raise questions about money being stolen from the union treasury. Department stores had already capitulated, letting Dave Beck organize their clerks under what he cynically called his American Plan to organize the employer instead of the employee.

---

[2] As befitting a secondary but still awesome status, the managing editor was entitled to a Small Window for his pet projects. The trinity of objects requiring sacred treatment was completed by an orange card indicating a Business Office Must. This was editorial copy promised to an advertiser, and was to get into the paper even if news had to be shoved aside to accommodate it.

Beck was a proper citizen and prominent Elk. Later a compliant Democratic governor was to make him a regent at my state university. Leading businessmen and the chamber of commerce were Beck's uneasy accomplices, either having made their accommodation with him, or fearing more Harry Bridges' longshoremen who were then marching inland from the waterfront. That titanic and bloody jurisdictional struggle between the craft unions and the invading toughs of Bridges' CIO was fought in the streets and alleys of Seattle as elsewhere.[3]

In his rage at Dave Beck, the General had made one understandable literary mistake. Beck surrounded himself with armed bodyguards but did not himself carry a weapon, and "Dave Beck's gun" became a vulnerable phrase when Beck sued for libel and won a large out-of-court settlement (it was twenty more years before Beck, through Bobby Kennedy's investigative efforts for a Senate committee, was finally put behind bars, and the teamsters got James R. Hoffa instead). After that costly experience with Beck, the *Times* muted its coverage of labor events in Seattle but devoted front page headlines repeatedly to obscure strikes in Michigan or North Carolina. This drip-drip method of presenting antilabor news became an obsession with the *Times*.

The undiscriminating way our paper condemned all unions, its constant playing down of any news that reflected favorably on President Roosevelt, its playing up of any innuendo against him from however untrustworthy a source,

---

[3] Newspapermen, forming their own union, had at first refused to link up with the labor movement, and called themselves a guild, in part out of elitist aloofness from blue-collar workers. But before long, in order to be economically effective against their employers, the guild joined the CIO. Full of New Deal sentiments, and mindful that I was less elitely paid than plumbers or linotype operators, I had no trouble thinking of myself as a workman. Not for me the spurious dignity of sandwiches hidden in briefcases; I bought the ugliest black lunch bucket I could find and toted it to work.

distressed me greatly at twenty-one. We didn't talk about such things around the city room, as we labored on the workaday minutiae that fill the American newspaper — the auto wrecks, the murders, the drownings, the city hall budget, the silver wedding anniversaries and tallest sunflowers. To this day I'm not even sure what our political editor's real beliefs were. This kindly old gentleman in years of Democratic landslides doggedly wrote predictions of Republican victories. He also wrote Sunday specials. Record numbers of state bureaucrats, he would report ominously, have been spotted taking their families out for Sunday drives in official cars. In the years when the Roosevelt administration was changing the face of America, and in Europe Hitler was locking up Jews and building up his armies, Joy-Riding in State-Owned Cars got our biggest Sunday headlines.

It is hard to measure now how effectual such distortions were in shaping public attitudes. But at the time they generated considerable passion on all sides. In college, I had admired Harold J. Laski's *Liberty in the Modern State,* so when this combative British socialist and scholar arrived in Seattle to lecture at the university, I asked to interview him. My story mostly quoted sympathetically Laski's admiration for his friend Felix Frankfurter, whose appointment to the Supreme Court had come over the wires that day. A week later, when the *Nation* reached Seattle with an article by Laski called "Why I Am a Marxist," he was no longer an obscure English labor party figure but an antichrist come to town to corrupt our youth.

The lumber baron whose will underwrote this annual lectureship must be turning in his grave, the *Times* lamented. A full "campaign" was ordered up, which meant that reporters were assigned to call up every pastor, priest, educator, Legion commander or club woman they knew, to report daily and mounting outbursts of staged indignation against Laski. That is, most other reporters got on the phone; my city editor never mentioned the subject to me and spared me the assignment.

The morning Hearst paper joined in the campaign, with only a little less fervor for being late. By now Laski was the most heard name in town. On the campus, where dislike of the *Times* was exceeded only by contempt for the Hearst paper, there rallied around Laski, not only the liberal elite who dominated academic life, but just about everybody who disliked the bullying tactics of the daily press.

Soon Laski's lectures had to be moved to the biggest auditorium on the campus, and I knew that *frisson* — not for the first time in my life, nor the last — of being among people who hated what I worked for, and myself secretly sharing some of their feelings. Those evenings were electric: Laski would wait until perhaps two-thirds of the way through his lecture before bringing the audience to life with a scathing passing reference to the local controversy. I'm not sure whether I'd be so impressed now; freedom of speech was indeed involved, in the sense that the timid might feel intimidated, but Laski himself was one of those cockfighters who enjoyed the appearance of martyrdom. I had not previously been exposed to that mixture of brilliance, fluency and arrogance one finds in English politicians, or to the malicious wit which is the courage of unprepossessing men. Laski's own reputation suffered later from the candor of his friends. But the experience was tingling then.

Deceiving memory will fasten its eye on some facet in the dark past that gleams now as it did not then. I suspect that I am making too much of my preoccupation with what took place in the ideological uplands of authority on my paper. Perhaps some personal shame persists. Around the city room all of us felt powerless to affect the paper's positions, and grateful to have work. What mattered, as we would have said then, was "to keep our own noses clean."

We were kept busy working under a pressure that ascended as each edition went to press. Even in the letup between deadlines, chatting among the staff was not encouraged; an assistant city editor would quickly descend with scutwork to do; if idle we had to feign busyness, and we muttered our asides like convicts. Nevertheless, we were a congenial crew, desk editors and reporters alike, and after hours gathered regularly in one another's homes for stag sessions of poverty poker, where in the interest of city room harmony the most anyone could lose in one night was two dollars. We thought ourselves the best staff in town, and in fact were capable of putting out a better paper. Once I asked the city editor why with all our resources and opportunities we didn't aspire to be ranked among the country's leading papers. He drily replied that our owners were making too much money to want our paper better.

Our total lack of curiosity about whatever shenanigans the proper people of our city were up to, our eagerness to misrepresent the views of those our paper disagreed with, our unwillingness to look unblinkingly at the disturbing side of our city — all this was part of the journalistic pattern of the times. In the unconfident atmosphere of the thirties editors even persuaded themselves that it was patriotic not to report the bad for fear it would lead to worse. As for political bias, our paper was a genteel offender compared to Hearst, to the Los Angeles *Times* or the Chicago *Tribune*. So much has everywhere changed — the Hearst press has gone tepid, the Los Angeles *Times* honest. My own paper was later to win its first Pulitzer Prize for showing how a university professor had been falsely accused of communism (earlier we wouldn't have cared).

HOW TRUE

The domineering old press lords of that day didn't get religion, they got competition. Not from one another, for as the number of metropolitan daily papers has shrunk, the majority of American cities now have one-ownership newspapers. What they lost, with the advent of radio, magazines and later of television, was their monopoly of access to the reader. As the old autocrats have died off, their papers have fallen into the hands of less despotic sons, family lawyers, or a new breed of publisher such as the rich businessman who runs one of the largest newspaper chains in the country and is indifferent to which party his paper in any city supports so long as it doesn't affect profits.

A lot of newspapermen are happy to have it this way; those who all along wanted less partisan reporting are now free — as on my old paper — to practice it. The docile servitude of the depression city room has disappeared. On many editorial pages, liberal and conservative views are carefully balanced in the choice of TV dinners of canned columnists. Editors, particularly in monopoly situations, feel such balancing an obligation. Even those crusty newspaper proprietors, whose outlook may be as crabbed as it ever was, judge it bad business to indulge their prejudices too overtly in print. They also usually want an untroubled relationship with any element in the community with enough leverage to be felt. It has become possible to write in well-modulated sociological prose of difficult matters like race and homosexuality, once subjects too hot to handle. All of this has meant a great improvement in the tone and temper of American daily journalism, along with a certain flatness. In the end, I think, papers should be judged, not by whether they fail to give offense, but by whether they fail to provide the news. And in many cities there remains an unwillingness to disturb, a reluctance to make waves, not because of a press lord's prejudices but from the counting room's prudence.

38

Nowadays the place to look for blatant twisting of the news, shoddy reporting and disregard for fairness is not in the Establishment press but in those who revile it — in the underground press or among those writers and magazine editors who have successfully copied the underground techniques in order to be trendy and with-it. The old press lords could ignore or defy the interests of their readers because of their own preponderant power and monopoly, and would often risk unpopularity out of a dogged adherence to their views. I find the new distorters a shrewd blend of opportunism, caprice and conviction: when they play fast and loose with the facts they do not so much go against the grain of their readership as play to its prejudices. Courageous is not the first word that comes to mind. (I suspect that young audiences may be somewhat indifferent anyway to the blur in the underground press between fantasy and fact, suspicious of any authority that professes to distinguish between them, and more fundamentally concerned with the vividness of the imagination and the echoing of their sentiments.)

I sometimes sigh, but not for long, for the gutsier, wrongheaded old journalism; I often admire the new journalism's exuberant pursuit of stories that others won't touch or don't have the wit to see. If only more American papers were willing to court unpopularity in the community by disturbing its complacent crust; if only the new journalists did not regard responsibility as a hindrance to their own creativity and abhorrent to their readership. Perhaps such a union of opposites — a respect for facts, married to imagination and passion — is not to be dreamed of; certainly it is rarely to be found. But it's the kind of journalism I stand and cheer for.

5

CHANGES

Journalism did a poor job of covering that era of multiple, unsettling changes, the 1960s. Journalism was flooded by change, was caught up in the novelty of it, lost its head and is still paying in a lack of public trust.

To be sure, much else suffered and suffers too in reputation; conventional wisdom proved insufficient for unconventional times. Yes, but journalism like a teapot handle is presumed to be able to remain cool while transmitting the hot.

So much happened so swiftly and reverberated so drastically that even now, after our own anguished participation in these times, after all the pictorial moments that are engraved on our brainpans, after the millions of words of arguments or explanation that we have been subjected to, we are still unclear what set off that explosive decade of the sixties. Nor do we yet fully comprehend about an era that is remembered for the violence of its confrontations, the lunacy of its assassinations, and the ugliness of its fears and hatreds, that relatively few lives were lost in all the tumult. Much was changed (mostly in people's heads) but much held. The story that journalism missed was the holding.

One notion that died in the decade, or should have, is that of simple cause and effect, the linearity of events. The unintended, the unforeseen, the fortuitous and the gratuitous predominated over the limited intentions of those who were prime movers of change, sometimes even giving them bigger victories than they envisioned or could cope with. Those who resisted change could not be said to be in control either. Nobody was.

A quantum leap in discontent took place in a nation that by any classical test was in no revolutionary mood, being more prosperous, and more responsible to the wishes of its people, than any other in history. What set it off? Does it all begin in the civil rights movement of the early Kennedy years, when the silent witness of thousands of peaceful marching blacks is met — on camera — by police dogs and water hoses, and when dedicated young college students go south to help intimidated rural blacks get the vote? Then how soon do the blacks, developing their own confidence, unexpectedly dismiss their white comrades, preferring with black pride to make it on their own? How soon, then, are the tactics and techniques learned in civil rights struggles transferred to other causes — finding at last, in resistance to the draft and to the war, issues that are both moral and pertinent to the students' own well-being? That was a volatile combination — the ghettos, the campus and the war — and it proved explosive.

But the alacrity with which ideas and tactics spread in that period owes most to television. I do not think it can be challenged that the networks, pursuing the highly visual, let their medium be captured by those who appeared on it. Television had to learn that it was not enough to turn cameras on the freakiest behavior and noisiest outcries on the ground that this was where the action was. Not when a television-wise generation had learned how to get attention by "symbolic violence," knew how to create disarray in the most pacific of gatherings, learned to wave placards that were unpaid commercials for their causes, and thus enjoyed coverage out of all proportion to their numbers or their importance.

Republicans later raised a great fuss about television's distorted news judgment, but Democrats have the real grievance. Those television editors who in Chicago in 1968 cut back and forth between rioters and the Democratic convention were — as Mark Antony said of Brutus — honorable men; certainly they had to act quickly in an unprecedented situation; but the pictorial linkage between the two events, and the confusion it left in the public's mind, was plainly a factor, and perhaps a deciding one, in Nixon's narrow victory in 1968.

Television editors had to learn (as I was to learn at *Life* magazine) that the camera has a bias for action. Judgment is required to correct this, and others will call the exercise of it bias, but judgment must be made. Yet against the power of the photograph, the most sensible of corrective words, written into captions or spoken off-camera by a newscaster, are feeble. The viewer's ear may ignore the explanation but his eye can't avoid the action.

Often, against the sense of its spoken words, television was in its commercials and in its programming spreading envy and awareness to all classes of people. Television news was teaching the young, the poor, and the discontented continuing examples of objectives gained through force, and success through effrontery. You might get busted, but you were on camera; so were the cops, so they had to be mindful.

It was teaching still others that the young were out of control, and black rage something to be feared; teaching that the education the elders had labored to make possible for the young had somehow gone wrong; that those in control — including college administrators — had abdicated authority, or weakly used it.

But of course the times were not all that linear either: what gave change its peculiar velocity in the 1960s was the unanticipated vulnerability of those in control, the way authority everywhere lost some of its self-confidence and command, and showed itself uncertain in response. Men who had been smoothly managerial behind barricades of secretaries and public relations handlers seemed less impressive when forced into the open.

Perhaps prior experience incapacitated them. For it was the young who, before anyone else, got the message of affluence, and made an appropriate response. (Their parents, who in their own youth had gotten the message of the depression, were still making responses appropriate to it.) On crowded campuses, herded together in treadmill classes, the young — mostly middle-class and white — discovered that in a period of affluence, with jobs around and parents to fall back upon, so relentless a preparation and pursuit of job security was no longer necessary. The compulsion of fear, so vivid to older minds, came across to the young as excessive counsel in the present. The lesson of affluence has since spread to everyone, even to those who claim to be most admiring of the work ethic, making workmanship less careful, service less attentive, discipline less binding.

As authority found itself called upon to explain, rather than merely to assert, its wisdom seemed less worthy of respect, its prerogatives less merited. Businessmen had to defend shoddy production and deceitful sales practices against Nader and other critics; and then answer for pollution, too. And in their own homes they found some of their most effective critics — not only their children but their wives. In that period everything seemed assailable, and just about everything was under attack.

What in American life deserved hanging onto, and would in any case be tenaciously defended, seemed less clear then, when the winds of change were gusting in unpredictable ways, than it does now. The winds of change may have shattered barometers, but they didn't abolish the pendulum. I think journalism failed to get its proportions right between the dynamic and preservative elements in society. The reason lies as much in two peculiarities of journalism as it does in conscious intent.

The first is a bias toward novelty. Journalism professes to tell you what the world is like, but in fact the real message of each day's newspaper is: this is what has *changed* in the world that you know about since last we reported to you. A journalist is in this respect something like a jazz soloist who assumes you already know the tune that he is playing variations upon. And if the newspaper describes a holdup last night on Beacon Street you are to assume, though the paper feels it unnecessary to say, that there were not similar holdups in hundreds of other peaceful streets.

The result of such omissions, however, is this picture of the world taken from one Sunday New York *Times:*

A bank closed because of embezzlement; a judge killed by criminals; grand jury indictments against prominent officials; reports on shoddy goods, unhonored warranties, cutthroat credit practices, more water, noise and solid-waste pollution; a hijacked plane; rising crime, public housing turned into a concentration camp for crime; senseless violence; muggings, a hospital spreading infections.

Speeches, interviews and complaints about drug traffic, corrupt police, discrimination, uncollected garbage, crowded courts, noxious air, traffic jams, protected monopolies, unworkable laws, official indifference, destruction of the countryside.

The distorting omission is of the ongoing and satisfactory. Page one is not a mirror of the world; it is the world with all the banality, the ordinary, the uncontroversial and the unchanging left out — that is, with most of the world's experience unnoted. "This is the way the world is," the editor will argue in defense of his page one. But is it? Or is this what is to be found by too absorbed a watch on the rat holes of trouble? You can't blame the editor for manning the danger spots: he is not culpable if he fails to anticipate the unexpected, but should be blamed if he has not prepared his readers for trends and events that might have been foreseen.

Disaster sells papers, it used to be said, but too much of it fatigues the spirit, so that reading the daily front page can become an unpleasant duty. Some editors seek to offset the gloom by devices as flimsy as "Today's Chuckle," or they set out to report "good news." Most such efforts strike me as labored, and readers rightly pass them by, detecting in them the absence of the hard earthiness of truth. Good news has first to be *news,* which is not apt to be found in an uncritical search for the reassuring. The real good news, if the mind is open to it, is in stories of people courageous against odds, standing up to pressure, asserting their humanity or cussedness, doing selfless acts, scoring quirky victories over circumstances. Such good news does not have to be labeled, merely recognized.

Television's antidote to its disturbing news, in the turbulence of the sixties, was usually applied in its off hours, when commentators and round-table panelists labored to offset the sheer vulgar force, or the partisan distortion, of what the camera had more excitingly shown. But I suspect that the more measured these efforts were, the less they were listened to. Journalists nevertheless kept at it, secure in their sense of acting responsibly, but knowing in their hearts how uphill the struggle was against the camera's bias for action, and journalism's fondness for novelty.

These two biases I believe to be at the heart of the valid criticism of journalism's performance in the 1960s, but the more familiar attack has been upon the opinions and emotional commitments of the journalists involved. Such journalistic subjectivity bears looking into. In the civil rights struggles in the south, when northern cameramen or reporters were as conspicuous by their presence and as unpopular as the demonstrators themselves, they shared a common jeopardy, which had to affect their reporting. But what I think really gave an edge of outrage to their coverage was the evidence of rights being ruthlessly denied.

That reportorial sense of injustice was, it seems to me, less evident in the campus disturbances, where demonstrations often had about them a sense of theatre and thrill, of seeing how far agitation could go until stopped. Grievances may have been real, and reforms overdue, but I never had much respect for those who on such grounds forcibly seized and messed up university buildings, then demanded amnesty for their actions — a travesty of the notion that one should be prepared to suffer for his convictions. Nor did I see the relevance in this context of quoting Fanon about Algeria, since his violent tactics were devised for situations where peaceful remedies were not available. I don't like hearing the language of those who have paid their dues on the lips of those who haven't. The fascist behavior of blocking Robert McNamara's car so that he could not speak at Harvard took a while to be called by its right name.

I remember once visiting an upstairs classroom "work-

46

shop" of Saul Alinsky's group in Chicago, where under the guidance of one of his organizers, eight or ten men and women in their twenties — brilliant, radical, and chilling in their own righteousness — talked about whether it would be more outrageous to stage a mass urination against the building of a public utility they despised, since its marble façade reminded them of a urinal anyway, or merely to "trash" the place, and in either event how to get maximum publicity.

Campus protests too depended on attracting television cameras; nevertheless, what made them journalistically ir-resistible was their ability to draw crowds that were sym-pathetic but not intensely so, relishing the put-down humor, and eager to see what the night would bring: would the cops behave too roughly, thus agitating the crowds against them; would the university president under pressure prove too stuffy, or lose his cool, or cave in? To the television generation, this was real-life theatre, and onlooker's sadism is a fine old American tradition.

The theatrical element in all of this was what journalism found hardest to handle: the situation may have been con-trived, but its consequences were actual, and how could one not cover a campus caught up in strife, and with random danger in the air? Besides, at such moments as the Cam-bodian invasion, passions were real. The killing at Kent State of four young onlookers by the guardsmen's panic response was tragic in itself; what made it shameful was the number of Americans who thought the dead students "had it coming to them," and resented the reporting that showed that some of the victims were not even demonstra-tors. (A journalist's bias can be tested against the evidence; the "consumer's" bias in what he refuses to hear or to credit is absolute.)

With placards and noise and calculated occupations of

forbidden space, demonstrators had found a way in the era of television to make opinions visible, and thus often to give them a false weight. Given the camera's bias for action, television's chief failure in this period was its withholding of responsible judgment, its failure to recognize that the presence of its cameras often provoked the trouble it professed merely to be the witness of. Its response to the chaos of the 1960s was just to get out of the way and let it all come at you. To this extent, television did its job all too graphically.

Its failure to mediate its coverage sufficiently came less, I think, from bias or sympathy with demonstrators than from a professional sense of discretion: a belief that "what is happening" should be shown straight, without any intervening efforts to guide viewers on how they should respond to it. In print journalism there are ways to distance oneself from any scene, or to put it in a larger setting. This is harder to do when the action is live, instantaneous and unpredictable — a situation that remains a core problem for television. Television's subsequent resolution of the problem — whether from timidity, in response to criticism, or out of a maturing sense of responsibility — has come at the expense of what moving cameras are intended for. Since newscasts have become mostly talking heads — with perhaps a still photograph or headline thrown upon the screen behind — television's attempts to give a feeling of place when it has no action to show looks merely foolish.[1] The result has been a diminution of the visualness of television's news coverage (which was television's initial advantage).

---

[1] I feel particular sympathy for those White House television reporters who, like all members of the press, get their news inside in the warmth of a briefing room, and could just as easily speak their piece in the comfort of a studio, but must don parkas and go out into the winter's cold so that their report can be unnaturally mouthed to the night air against the dramatic backdrop of the lighted White House.

The gain has been the elimination of pseudo-events which became "news" only because of the camera's presence.

Just as police, against the grain of their instincts, learned that riots were more effectively controlled by disciplined police work rather than by cracking heads, so journalists in the 1960s developed more sophistication about who had a right to be seen and heard, and with what frequency. They freed themselves from the merely noisy — but took a while to discover the silent.

Was this because of a lack of sympathy with the silent? Perhaps, but more fundamental, I think, is another hazard that is present in the way that journalism does its job, which is its gravitation toward the articulate. As many journalists have cause to know, you can get into trouble guessing what people may be thinking when they aren't saying. (I remember the entire American press in 1948, puzzling over how Truman could be drawing such crowds when the polls and experts knew for sure Dewey was going to win. And so those crowds had to be explained away by the experts. *Time* magazine, where I then worked, reported knowingly that Truman's crowds came out only from curiosity to see a cocky little fighter.)

If the entire American press, caught up on the confused and exciting recording of change, was slow to detect and report another kind of change — that of a developing resistance to the new and a holding onto the old — this happened in part because the mood was slow to find its voice. But journalism misunderstood it when it did.

It seemed to be the voice of Archie Bunker's America, without benefit of a scriptwriter's reassuring evasions. That side of American life, as Gibbon said of Corsica, is easier to deplore than to describe. Its prejudices were so familiar as not to seem news. I remember sensing on *Life* magazine an imbalance which seemed hard to correct. Journalism everywhere was reporting the Get Whitey rhetoric of black prejudice, finding it a fresh discovery about people whose feelings had not previously been listened to. But journalism, ours included, hesitated to quote anti-niggerism in Polish and Italian neighborhoods, either because the language and thought seemed as tediously old as the Ku Klux Klan, or because we thought we should not add to racial tension.

A similar hesitance to speak out, an inability to find the words for feelings strongly held, was what became known as silence in a large public. It was not merely Archie Bunkerism. In poll after poll a majority has shown that it completely accepts desegregation in public places and transportation, and believes in equal education for blacks. But this majority's worries about other issues which had a black context to them (taxes, welfare, schools, drugs, crime) it found hard to express, except to friends or in the privacy of the voting booths. After all, these Americans found it hard enough even to talk about *blacks* (colored, the word they were used to, seemed politer, less pejorative). Their fears of crime, of deteriorating neighborhoods and unsafe environments were too easily branded as racism. They recognized the shrewd perception of George Wallace that many of those who acted superior to ordinary people's concerns were Washington congressmen, journalists, academics, and the "radical chic," who themselves could afford to live in inviolate neighborhoods and to send their children to private schools. The silent majority (a description that may not fit but is irritatingly useful) also found that many of the accumulated follies of our times came from the assertive clamor of the intellectuals, and for this intuition were denounced as anti-intellectuals. The frustrations of having legitimate concerns dismissed as prejudices is part of the legacy of the 1960s. Journalism missed this story, I believe, largely through a withholding of sympathy that would have produced understanding. Politicians like Wallace, Agnew and Nixon found code words to signal their support of these positions, and were the gainers. Journalism was slow to, and suffered.

6

ATTITUDES

To choose a career is to choose how life is going to happen to you. As long ago as I can remember I wanted to be a journalist. While my schoolmates were wise in hubcaps and fender treatments that marked this year's Buick from last, I studied the characters of whatever newspapers I could lay hands on, and found romantic the very type-shapes of their front page logotypes — the proud Gothic dignity of the New York *Times,* the plain square-cut legend of the Kansas City *Star,* and the brassy patriotism of any Hearst paper, its name enwrapped in American flags while from a ferocious eagle's beak trailed ribbons improbably celebrating patriotism, freedom and truth.

If every choice of career is a limiting, it is in the beginning a freedom, a zest of potentialities. Just as in that other crucial romantic decision of one's life — that of marriage

— one acts with a show of reason but under the ordering of illusion.

I thought journalism meant to live in the actual, to see and then to describe, to seek the truth, to show the way. Other careers might be valuable, but to me too *narrow,* insufficiently encompassing, too physical, beyond me (music or mathematics), too messy (labs), too routine (office work), unworthy (public relations), selfish (business), false (selling), fusty (scholarship). Illusion sustained me through the apprentice discovery of how dull, grubby and trivial much of journalism can be; sustained me until I became surer again that journalism was where I was meant to be.

As a boy, my favorite short story had been *Gallagher,* written by a swashbuckling newspaperman named Richard Harding Davis. Its details are no longer vivid to me, only its impact. Gallagher was an office boy who chanced on a raging fire, with no one present from his paper to cover it. He carefully got all the facts and then set off for the office in his horse and carriage (the story was vintage pre–World War I), urging on his steed through the night, arriving breathlessly at the editor's office with the news. Other boys might stir to air duels in Spads over the German lines, or to a lawyer's brilliant summation that freed a frail, innocent girl. Gallagher the fire-chaser was my hero.

Only after some years of practicing the same trade did I think back on this childhood story and make a surprising discovery: it was the *fire fighters,* and not Gallagher, who had been in the heat of the action. For all his derring-do in racing back to the newspaper, Gallagher had not been a participant but a witness, a conveyer, a describer. Others do; a journalist watches.

It was a voyeur's trade I was in, with some of the voyeur's advantages: a journalist doesn't have to take part, isn't in the spotlight, doesn't have to think up the appropriate spur of the moment retort, explain his behavior, do the fighting, take the heat. Being on the scene, knowing the participants, he develops friendships, sympathies and dislikes. But by not enlisting in causes, he is free of having to think of what he himself would do in any circumstance; by belonging to no organization, he feels little responsibility for results, feels no pull of loyalty to defend, as others must, what they are part of. If his field is politics or foreign affairs, he is professionally caught up in the arguments of the moment, but only if he is an analyst or a columnist is he expected to make independent sense of them. So while critics fret about a journalist's subjectivity getting in his way, I find myself more concerned about an emotional detachment in a journalist that can easily become insensitivity, a withholding of judgment that can easily become a mindless indifference to other people's aspirations.

Such self-isolation, the habit of nonmembership in society's groupings, leaves me cool toward many forms of public enthusiasm. I find myself fidgeting during displays of cocktail hour idealism of the kind quite marked in the campaigns of Adlai Stevenson, Eugene McCarthy and George McGovern, which aspires to rally together all the "good people" against the forces of darkness. It doesn't take cynicism in the journalist to know that few lives are pure though some deeds may be; that victories are made by achieving majorities with diverse motives, in which the hope of gain, the pull of ambition, the force of habit and the degree of concern may be impossible to sort out. The end may not justify the means, but it often justifies the alliances. "All there is to public statesmanship," Abraham Lincoln insisted, "is controlling and directing *individual meanness* for the public good." I feel safer in any controversy where there are men with *interested* motives on both sides, when a cause is not exclusively the property of those who judge the merit of an argument by the presumed sincerity of the feelings involved (for such people it is always enough for the heart to be in the right place); not exclusively the property of those who constantly find every proposed solution inadequate in the light of some ideal; or of those who find in political causes an external parallel to their personal discontents.

My own civic passivity also makes me suspicious of several other modes of public enthusiasm:

Retroactive superiority, which is an attitude endemic in the young but not confined to them. This is the mentality that looks back and finds Lincoln a racist because he didn't anticipate the Civil Rights Act of 1964. In recent years, the worst example of retroactive superiority has been the contempt of militant blacks for the "Uncle Toms" of the immediately preceding generation, that remarkable group of men, including Jackie Robinson, Ralph Bunche, Gordon Parks and Roy Wilkins, who by their achievements won a precarious acceptance in white society, an acceptance that at any moment could be put in jeopardy, even in hailing a cab. Most of these "Toms" ended up psychologically bruised as well as toughened, and their courageous survival in so ambivalent a setting prepared the way for what has come after them.

Safe courage. To be the most strident denouncer of the British in Irish South Boston or the stoutest enemy of the Arabs in a Jewish neighborhood is asking to be measured on a decibel chart that I have little respect for. Outspokenness of opinion, to be admired, requires, I think, some personal cost or risk, just as courts give special weight to testimony that is called "admission against interest."

Middle-ground superiority. "There is much to be said on both sides" is usually voiced with judicious gravity, but the calm of reasonable men often comes from the fact that their own interests are not involved, or they themselves are not the victims of injustice. (The journalist's "neutrality" is often no more than this.) Whenever I hear the comfortable refrain that politics is the art of the possible, I suspect the speaker of an unwillingness to chance the possible, thereby ensuring its impossibility.

The noble victim fallacy, or the illusion that the victims of society hold the same values as those who go to their aid. When this later proves not to be the case, complaints of ingratitude get heard. During the depression, all New Dealers (I counted myself one) thought of themselves as the pure at heart because they were the have-nots; bigotry and selfishness resided exclusively in the haves. But the Okies of the *Grapes of Wrath* era were, in their hard-won California prosperity, to prove themselves unmoved by the downtrodden Chicanos of a later era; labor unions born of struggle and brotherhood became exclusive clubs to keep out those on the next rung below; and minorities risen to power quickly became disregarding of the rights of others without power. The impulse to help others to gain their rights or to get a better break is crucial to making democracy work. Still, the victim you help may be your ally this time, but not the next.

These judgments may be experienced wisdom, but I acknowledge that they also may merely be a weary finickiness in a sardonic onlooker. Having staked out a journalist's need and right to be independent, having decided that I vote but do not join, I at some point lost the ability to use the word "we" in the sense of "all those who feel as I do," that language that comes so naturally to the tongue of people who exhort others, who feel themselves members of a group with a common cause to further or interests to defend. And though from the sidelines it is easy enough to belittle the excesses of the activists, I frequently envy them their achievements and their passion.

In disasters, a journalist sometimes shares danger, but as witness, not helper — he doesn't aid the victim, chase the bandit or return the gunfire. But, like other professionals, he learns to deaden reactions which get in the way of doing his job — a disengagement at the crucial moment from feelings people normally have. As with a surgeon, a policeman or an accountant, what is important to the craft is often accomplished at some expense to the self. *Hard hats must be worn in this area.*[1]

More troubling for the roundedness of a journalist's character is the limitations his craft puts on the development of his own ideas. Unless he is himself a specialist, a journalist is apt to be interested in any subject about as much and as long as the public is (to be expert in the present in all its variety can also make you shallow about everything else). He spends so much time expounding other people's ideas that he has too little time to discover his own. A good interviewer learns to listen, not to trade opinions with his source — on the job his own ideas exist as a primer to draw out the views of another. His head is an anthology of borrowed opinions, which he sometimes tries to reconcile. He learns to restrain his own prejudices: he must count the crowds fairly and quote the best lines of the man he doesn't like. A journalist knows himself not to be a solver (if his scent tells him something is wrong, he will be able to find others more vocal than he to deplore it, others more knowledgeable than he to remedy it). Having access to people with expertise in

---

[1] As a cub police reporter I resolved to conquer squeamishness, and to steel myself, deliberately chose to watch a particularly grisly autopsy, that of ten-year-old twin boys whose father had shot them in the head. After that appalling afternoon I decided to let ugly experiences seek me out.

a subject, he is apt to be more modest about the worth of his own uninstructed insights, and loses some of that carefree American dogmatism about any and all subjects. That's why those bespectacled Washington correspondents are such solemn-looking fellows.

He fears becoming a partisan, a crank or a bore on any subject, and thereby professionally disabled. A journalist must be more seized by journalism than by any subject it deals with. Most journalists hang a little loose in their thinking. They are fated to have to listen to both sides of every argument (and may be the last people in the country who do). They content themselves with sharp judgments about persons but only vague attitudes about correct policy. Don't ask journalists for finished philosophy; they have spent their professional lives fighting off the temptation.

A journalist, like a soldier, develops some service-connected disabilities. From the start, he is determined to lose his naïveté quickly, and expects to meet phonies and self-servers; but more disillusioning is the discovery of well-intentioned people who cannot be trusted. He becomes less categorical about who in public life belongs in outer darkness, as he learns that honor and character are more evenly divided among men of opposing political views than once he thought.

He has been subjected to too many glamorous or aggressive egos, covered too many speeches, listened to too many rhetorical jury pleas, seen money and respectability corrupt too many lives, seen so many experts confounded by their ignorance, seen so many sure things go wrong, seen too much piety that is merely a mask for selfish concerns. Imperfection is the journalist's working climate. He is leery of the rhapsodical. He becomes hesitant in avowing his own idealism, which may only survive in the stubborn conviction that the truth matters. But about this he is not passive, and in his sedentary way plays the tiger. He is a skeptic who hopes to avoid cynicism.

Such qualities need not incapacitate him, but do help to define him. He is neither defender of any faith nor prophet of new orders, nothing so grand as that. His role in society is more like a dredging engineer, whose job it is to keep channels free and clear. A journalist watches the currents of society closely, and acts when he sees the channel silting up, or its course deflected. His concern is always with the now and with what comes next; he is not interested in repeating what has already been told; his delight is in discerning the new and then making it clearer. Discovery is his job. To it, he hopes to bring a combination of knowledge and innocence, so that in confronting the new, he can be well-prepared yet also fresh-eyed and unburdened.

7

Memory Cell:
TIME

There was always something electric about *Time* magazine in the old days. It wasn't neutral, and people weren't neutral about it. Many of the leading writers of the day had at one time or another worked for it, but there were others, such as Edmund Wilson, who regarded its views, its presumptions and its prose, its mood of "jeering rancor" with as much distaste as I had earlier felt for the Hearst press.

But for me, a young man from Seattle, *Time* magazine was the place where I most wanted to work. As assistant city editor of the Seattle *Times,* I had a good job, but its routines and limited horizons frustrated me; I wanted to be concerned with national politics and foreign affairs more than with Today's Traffic Lesson. In between had come a year as a Nieman Fellow in journalism, where I was exposed to the dialectical flash of Harvard professors and the comradeship of a dozen other newspapermen from all over the

country, and found my pent-up political prejudices rein-
forced — always a dangerously comfortable experience for
me. I work better professionally when my views are
crowded and challenged, for I recognize that out of antagonism comes quality, which is why the best sculptures are of
marble, not of soap. The danger of accommodation to what
you are at war with is less to be feared than the intellectual
laxity that seizes you when you are preaching to the already
converted.

I admired the economy and cleverness of *Time* writing
more than I was distressed by its mannerisms. Its prose
didn't bother me as much as it did Edmund Wilson, since I
had worse newspaper habits to unlearn. I wanted to join
such clever company, and wanted to write for an audience
quick enough to respond to it. The *Time* slant, as it was
then called, loomed as a problem — would I be expected to
write against my own views? — but that could wait to be
faced.

I had been asked how much I expected to be paid, mum-
bled that I would leave it to them, and was offered 50 percent more than I would have dared ask for. But I was one
of three men newly hired on three months' trial, after which
there would be a job for only one of us. I was thus leaving
behind the plains of American working life, the undemanding world of post office employees, craft unions and factory
shifts, of places where men work side by side easily and do
not try to best one another. I was shown to a closet-sized
office, which I shared with one of the other writers trying
out; he later became a distinguished professor, but at this
moment felt so competitive that when I asked him that first
day how one got a supply of pencils here, he wouldn't tell me.

Lunches were the big moment at *Time*. After a morning
spent in sedentary isolation staring at a typewriter, hoping to
collapse mountains of clippings and research into a bright

two or three paragraphs — frustrating, bedeviling labor that seemed so easy and could be so difficult — we would come out of our little warrens around one o'clock. Usually we would head off for Lindy's on Broadway, perhaps a half-dozen of us, and over a martini and an outsized delicatessen sandwich would high-spiritedly dispute for an hour and a half, before carefully splitting the check and returning to our cells. The conversation was fast and sharp, the kidding of each other's strengths and weaknesses relentless; we leapt from topic to topic, and woe to the man who lingered too long or felt it necessary to display expertise; the wit wasn't as prepared and well-turned as at the Algonquin Round Table (which I'm sure had its dull moments too) but lived in its topicality and spontaneity. I liked these worldly fellows, but sat close-mouthed among them until I too learned the put-down art that felt sympathy but never expressed it, stated passionately held views but phrased them lightly. We were murderously corrective of any signs of vanity in one another, yet really valued each other's passing praise in the corridor more than our editors' approval.

After a year and a half of this clubby, collective wrestling with the affairs of state and the state of Harry Luce's soul, I was moved to the individualistic world of the "back of the book" cultural departments, which were manned by gifted, independent and idiosyncratic writers who weren't in the least clubbable and disdained the polemical heavy breathing up front. Louis Kronenberger covered theatre, and in stately eighteenth-century cadenced sentences wrote reviews that were exactly forty-three lines long — precisely calibrated to fit one illustrated column of text — and on this heavily re-written magazine was furious if any editor presumed to alter a sentence. Walker Evans was a writer who had earlier made a reputation for spare, uncompromising photographs that were the enemy of all that is arty. As a writer he was the irascible opponent of that forced sharpening of judgment, either in praise or attack, that was basic to *Time* style. James Agee, who had collaborated with Evans on *Let Us Now Praise Famous Men,* was a hulking mountain man whom Harvard never tamed nor *Time* domesticated — a marvelous luncheon companion, gentle, brilliant and unkempt. (The managing editor regarded it as a wonder of nature that Agee seemed always to show up for work with a *two day* growth of beard.) I liked hearing Agee describe how Beethoven's last quartets were slowly yielding their secrets to him, like great granite cliffs gradually crumbling, or describing with a characteristic shaping gesture of both hands, as if carefully carving a walnut, how a movie director achieved an effect. Often we talked of religion. Religious quarrels had divided my family as a child and had left me without faith, conscious of missing a solace and authority that meant so much to others. Such star *Time* writers as Agee, Nigel Dennis and Alwyn Lee were deeply read in theology and eloquent in refutation, but unable to escape its fascination. Their heavens, hells and purgatories would have been unrecognizable to Harry Luce, as Luce's and John Foster Dulles's religious statecraft would have been to them.

Soon I was put to editing, and at the age of twenty-eight was the youngest editor on *Time.* It is true, as Calvin Trillin has written about *Time,* that in its highly processed series of editings, the last person with any say is apt to be the one with the least familiarity with the facts. Still, it is both possible and necessary to edit people who may be more knowledgeable than you, just as one can interview experts and report their views. An editor's job is to ask the questions that a reader would, to simplify and cut, or to urge the writer to try it another way. Much of editing is really about how long things should be. Furthermore, we had an uneven staff, and even the best of writers have their bad weeks. "Only mediocrity," Max Beerbohm has said, "can be trusted to be always at its best."

On occasion it fell to me to edit Agee's movie reviews, a prospect that would have been more intimidating had he not generally been so tolerant, and even grateful, for editing. He wrote five times as much as he knew we had space for but often wrote one paragraph making a point, then without crossing it out came at the same point in a different way, and his editor had only to make the choice Agee had been unwilling to. More often I was editing the book reviews of such men as Nigel Dennis, Robert Fitzgerald, Robert Cantwell, Irving Howe and Max Gissen — an impressive array of obstinate talents. I was learning from them while editing them; in fact, *Time* was to be a postgraduate education for me, and on days off there were the theatres, museums and bookshops of Manhattan in which to complete my lab work.

In T. S. Matthews, Luce had had the temerity to choose a literary man as his managing editor. Tom Matthews was determined to rid *Time* of its cheap, smart-alecky and dated mannerisms and was savage on clubfooted writing, but since he had his own gift for elegant malice, in the end the magazine under him did not become detectably more lovable. Matthews, though the best editor I have ever known, had the sentimental notion that writers, not editors, were the heart of the magazine, and invited his writers to express themselves on the point. He got hearty agreement from Paul O'Neil, who came from the same Seattle paper I did and was the writer most admired by his fellow writers at *Time*. In response to Matthews's request Paul struck a chord on his "splintered mandolin" to sing a few stanzas about "that nervous gladiator, the *Time* writer":

The world knows little about him, and what it does is generally incorrect. It is true that somebody in Corporate sometimes grabs one of him and holds him up to the pink window of the Publisher's Letter for the readers to see . . . and the world is given the impression that he has just got back from Yucatan with a tan, and is going off to see Churchill as soon as he has lunch with Lana Turner at the Stork Club.

Actually he is an anxious looking fellow with thinning hair, whose stomach has the knobby rigidity of a Mexican gourd from eating too much Union News food. He spends his days crouching in the blue-tinted horror of his writing hutch, like an incorrigible in solitary, fumbling with paper and hating himself. He never sees the outer world — he is forcefed by paper. Occasionally he takes a pill. Occasionally he glares wildly out the window. But mostly he sits humped over his typewriter, smoking cigarettes and throwing them on the floor and staring morosely at the wall. He is waiting for his brains to work.

He is a kind of word mechanic who must yank odd shaped chunks of raw fact off the overhead belt, trim it to size (often with his teeth) assemble his jig saw of conflicting information into something with a beginning, a middle and an end, bolt the whole together with adjectives, and send it through the hopper, glittering, polished and blushing with jeweler's rouge. . . . He is eternally surrounded by a ragged circle of secondary characters, buzzard-like creatures who waddle towards him with venal beaks and peck him cruelly when he begins to concentrate. Researchers — young women with enormous egos and a minimum of judgment — shrill at him from ink stained mouths.

Like the club fighter, whose work is that of getting his ears scrambled once a fortnight at St. Nicholas Arena, the Time writer has his points. He is durable and cunning. It is my contention that he is a unique and valuable fellow. I am inclined to believe that the theory of Group Journalism is highly overrated, and that the brigades of editors, researchers, advisers and assorted double-domers who are popularly believed to be helping the writer are actually just riding around on his back, shooting at parakeets, waving to their friends, and plucking fruit from overhanging branches while he churns unsteadily through the swamps of fact and rumor with his big, dirty feet up to the knee at every step.

One of my chores was to edit the section Matthews cared most about, Books. His one-sentence directive to me was impossibly pure: in the course of a year, *Time* should not overpraise the bad books, or undervalue the good. Matthews was exactingly discontent and kept our standards high. From him I came to appreciate that (in Virginia Woolf's words) "to give praise its meaning the standard of the first rate must be present in the mind, unconfused and unlowered." I also came to recognize that the converse of this could be found in a remark of Coleridge's: "Praises of the unworthy are felt by ardent minds as robberies of the deserving." My mind still ardently believes that, and suffers dourly the routine over-praise that one hears in television palavering.

Tom Matthews wanted a book section comparable to the best English literary reviews; Harry Luce wanted a news section about books, with particular emphasis on best sellers. Tom's era as managing editor was drawing to an end, and I was sometimes present at testy small lunches with them when the disagreement seemed to be about this but was really about so much else. I innocently thought both were right and could be satisfied. Why shouldn't a book section correctly esteem books of quality while taking note of best sellers? Unfortunately, in our reviewers' hands, to "take note" of best sellers was to invite a succession of merciless slash jobs, which was not what Luce had in mind. In this our reviewers were often right, but unduly vindictive. They felt themselves guardians of the kingdom of literature against the middlebrows at the gates. These were men to whom literature mattered, and I envied them their stock of reading beyond the kind of practical journalistic information I was read in, which was useful for the moment but of little residue; they were at ease in the frivolities of Firbank and the poetry of Yeats; the commercial confection of best sellers held little interest for them.

Reviewing, it must be admitted, is parasitical and therefore frustrating work; good appreciations are harder to come by than facile demolitions. I made two discoveries: that reviewers are frequently hardest on the kind of book they wish they had written themselves; and that, though they take genuine pleasure in discovering a promising writer, if asked to review a first novel that someone else has already discovered, they invariably write reviews asking what the fuss is all about.

In one afternoon's work, a reviewer can demolish or dismiss a year's effort by an author, and something about *Time*'s cocksure style encouraged wit at the expense of the work. The reader had to be served, to be jogged awake by facile writing and swift judgment. Since so many published books are hackwork or junk, some reviewers thought of themselves as public defenders. They would crib what was most interesting in the book, then suggest that there was no need to read more than that of it. What I respected most in critics like Agee, Fitzgerald and Howe was their creative sympathy for what a writer or a movie director was trying to do, and their effort to guide the reader to recognize, savor and celebrate quality.

Time's elaborate system of cross-checks and back-ups was designed to allow on-the-job training, even of editors. But it also encouraged, along with the need to learn, a need to sound as if you already knew. I was thus undergoing a forced self-education with a quick pass-along to the readers — dealing in reflections for immediate delivery. Generally I forbore to impose my critical opinions on writers who knew their subject better, but had I then known more about their fields, I would have edited better. I remember with regret

that all during that golden postwar era in American painting, when the abstract expressionists shifted the art capital of
the world from Paris to New York, *Time* reported their
achievements with eloquent scorn or feeble praise, written
by a gusty fellow whose only genuine enthusiasms among
contemporary painters were Edward Hopper and Charles
Burchfield. As his editor, I wish I had confidently known
that there was so much more around to be admired than
that.

Then it came time for me to return to politics again.
Time's misjudgment of the 1948 Truman election had been
no worse than that of the rest of the American press; perhaps
Time felt so certain of Dewey's election that it felt little need
to display its Republican bent too brazenly. But Matthews
as managing editor seized the occasion to change editors,
and to put me in charge of national affairs. There followed
an agonizing year and a half of my life, for *Time* was soon
to have another managing editor, Roy Alexander, and it became evident that Luce wanted his Republicanism more
explicit in the magazine. I wasn't the man for that.

The political tensions at *Time* are part of journalistic
legend, and the source of several flawed novels and films.
Perhaps the situation is impossible to describe, and I shall
fail too. But in this contest of wills between forceful and
ambitious people are all the elements of the debate about
the press that is going on today. It was not simply a Mani-
chaean contest between darkness and light, but a continuing
struggle between a man who had invented a new kind of
journalism and was its owner and felt he could do with it
whatever he wanted, and those he had hired who had their
own strongly held notions about any journalism they were
going to be a part of, and had as their only weapons their
talents, their arguments and their readiness to leave. Men

like Matthews, John Hersey and Theodore H. White broke with Luce with good cause, but I have read others whose self-described heroic defiances — their refusals to write the story that would have started World War III — are unrecognizable to me. A recent biographer of *Time,* W. A. Swanberg, not much at home in contemporary affairs, has solved the problem of conflicting testimony by regarding as credible witnesses only those who left Luce's employ, for whatever reason, and thus gets much wrong.

The outspokenness of *Time* was its attraction for those who worked on the magazine as well as for those who read it. So people who went there to work were already converts to its methods, or already compromised, if you feel, as McGeorge Bundy once expressed it, that *Time* "badly fudged the line between reporting and judging." In its weekly compression, *Time* had no room for long newspaper columns of details, and somewhere else an editorial opinion. All this was to be bound together for the busy reader, who in one evening's reading was promised everything he needed to know about the week past. That ambition reflects the callow audacity of young men out of the more naïve and simpler days of Harding. With newspaper clippings, a few reference books and a bag of literary tricks they would make the whole world plain, and fun to read about too (quizzes were big in the early *Time*). As the world got more complex, Briton Hadden and Luce became less satisfied with quoting or debunking other people's opinions, and developed views of their own. Soon they had their own correspondents in the field, and had to reckon with their judgments too. And to deal with the real world of finance or art or science at a level beyond flip dismissal, they had to get better and more responsible writers. The risk was that responsibility would bring on dullness; a wisecrack was no longer enough for a conclusion; the wit had to be in the brevity.

Luce knew that he couldn't put out the lively magazine he wanted if everyone wrote to order. Most of the writers on *Time* would have then described themselves as liberals, a category that has since lost most of its glamor and much of its meaning. They came not just for the salaries (which is the only reason uncomprehending historians can find to account for Luce's acknowledged ability to hire good men); nor did they come with a realistic hope of seizing the ship, for this was not possible. They were attracted by the *Time* invention, and the chance to put their own views before a large audience. Confident judgments supported by the facts was what was wanted. For men who felt cramped elsewhere, here was an invitation to say plainly what they felt.

Luce was thus inviting his own problems, and of course knew it. He was full of such ambivalences; he wanted to prevail, but respected independence, disliked trimmers and was bored by those whose opinions suspiciously echoed his, though he might for a time find them useful. He was something like a tennis player who wants victory, but only after a hard-fought match. I early learned not to write defensively against Luce's known prejudices, for the result always failed in its wishy-washyness. Best to write as forcefully as you could what you thought was right, counting on your facts to carry the day. I've come to believe that most arguments (whether in print or at dinner parties) are usually not about facts, which may not even be in dispute, but about *projections* of what will happen because of them. The unprovability of the assertion is what makes the argument. For some minds, well confirmed in their liberal views and enveloped in their own certainty, this contesting of attitudes was intolerable. Some tried sly tricks. A writer on *Life* was much admired by some when he diminished the effect of a laudatory article on Dewey by noting deadpan in a picture caption that Dewey, at his governor's desk, was sitting on a telephone book to increase his height. Not often did writers score so spectacularly on editors who were themselves adroit in words. Other writers with decided political views took refuge in unpolitical back of the book sections,[1] where from positions of safety they scornfully derided us who occupied "the bloody angle" of national affairs.

I suppose it was possible to write "the line" cynically, and perhaps some writers with big families to support did, but never successfully for long. Something about the flat-out character of *Time* writing made it hard to fudge your opinions or to be casual about them; conclusions had to be drawn, and the process exposed most efforts to blur or weasel. Most writers cared very much, which made *Time* a stimulating and feisty place. Most could say, as can I, that though I would later come to regard something I had written as unfair or wrong, I have never consciously written anything which at the time I thought to be untrue. This may seem an immodest boast; it actually is a minimum condition for any journalism that a reader can trust, or a writer can take pride in. The accommodating process has something in common with Justice Robert Jackson's description of writing a majority opinion on the Supreme Court: to him dissenting or concurring opinions were more enjoyable to write, because "when you're writing for the Court, you try to bring your view within the limits of the views of all those who are supporting you. That often requires that you temper down your views to suit someone who isn't quite as convinced as you, or who has somewhat different grounds." Around *Time* that process was called, unfondly, "group journalism."

In the 1930s, long before I arrived on the scene, Luce had begun to find in the Republican party a suitable vehicle for his crusading spirit. That got in the way of his journalism,

[1] There, however, other quarrels existed. The science editor didn't care how much his section was cut, just so that it got more space than religion.

though I think most Republican leaders regarded him as a maverick never quite to be trusted, for in any real test, they felt, his journalistic independence would win out. It frequently did, but not always. And out of this characteristic ambiguity in Luce came much of the drama of working at *Time*.

At the beginning of the 1950s, the "bloody angle" at *Time* was not a pleasant trench to be in. China, the land where Luce was born to a missionary family, had fallen to the Communists in 1949; his friend Chiang Kai-shek had fled to Formosa, and Luce was unable to accept this turn of events as solely Chinese in origin. He was always contemptuous of Senator Joe McCarthy — contemptuous enough to take him less seriously than others did, regarding him as a bungler and a liar, and Luce couldn't understand people too timid to stand up to him. But McCarthy, looking for targets on whom to hang the demagogue's charge of treason, settled on people whom Luce did not regard as traitors, but did think had contributed by inaction or misjudgment to the fall of China. *Time*'s effort to demonstrate how reckless were McCarthy's charges was sometimes hampered by Luce's disapproval of the men McCarthy was after. George Marshall, that most upright and respected of all our soldiers in World War II, could hardly get a favorable mention in *Time* after what Luce regarded as the gullibility of Marshall's postwar mission to China. Dean Acheson was suspect for refusing to turn his back on his friend Alger Hiss, whom *Time*'s own Whittaker Chambers had accused of espionage for the Russians.[2] It is an irony that Richard Nixon must savor that

[2] Chambers, a strange, secretive man, brilliant but mystic and warped, had been foreign editor of *Time*, a job I was to succeed to some years later. Most of the legitimate complaints by disaffected writers about how their copy was tampered with at *Time*, and the evidence of their facts callously disregarded, come from his tenure. He had a considerable intellectual influence on Luce, and is the reason *Time* escaped the common euphoria about the postwar good intentions of Stalin's Russia. Some of

Acheson should come to be regarded by revisionist historians as the most ardent of cold-war diplomats. Perhaps they weren't around for Nixon's attacks on Dean Acheson's Cowardly College of Communist Appeasers.

It was in that trying period — of McCarthy, Korea, the Hiss-Chambers trial and General MacArthur's recall — that I edited *Time*'s national affairs section, with as capable a staff of writers as I think the magazine ever had.[3] We had the easy indolent pride and confidence in our abilities that championship teams have, and only this enabled us to endure a period that in memory seems most marked by tiredness; too many nights till 3 A.M., too many cigarettes, too much coffee.

Alexander, the new managing editor, was a jovial and earthy ex-newspaperman whom we all enjoyed drinking and eating with at Toots Shor's, where he commanded a favorite's head table. Alex had been one of the first Irish Catholics to turn from New Deal liberalism on the issue of communism, and he became increasingly impatient with those he thought muddled or naïve on the subject.

Matters came to a head during the Korean War, when Truman recalled General Douglas MacArthur for insubor-

---

Chambers's partisans thought that Luce treated him shabbily by forcing his resignation during the Hiss-Chambers case. I never thought so. Chambers joined *Time* as an avowed ex-Communist turned passionate crusader against communism, but never admitting that he had been a Soviet courier guilty of espionage. My own distaste for him was more professional: however genuine his convictions, I thought him a dishonest journalist.

[3] In those days without by-lines their best work remains anonymous. Some are less anonymous now but all deserve a retroactive salute: Edward Cerf; Duncan Norton-Taylor (later managing editor of *Fortune*); Robert Manning (later editor of *The Atlantic Monthly*); A. T. Baker (later a *Time* senior editor); Paul O'Neil; Louis Banks (later editorial director of Time Incorporated); James Keogh (later Nixon's director of the U.S.I.A.); and, for various periods, novelist Joe David Brown and Gilbert Millstein. It had its own balance of liberals and conservatives. Besides good ensemble work, each was capable of enlivening solos.

dination. Luce went to call on the general at the Waldorf, got tears in his eyes in his presence, and later pressed on him a million dollars for his memoirs in *Life*. On our magazine, Luce and Alexander gave the foreign editor his head in eulogizing MacArthur, and he proceeded to characterize Truman's recall of MacArthur as a step that "brings World War III closer." In my own national affairs section, we found it hard to report the news with any evenhandedness or fairness to the President, without seeming inconsistent with what followed. I had always thought it a duty in editing never to subject the magazine to deadly side-by-side quotation of *Time*'s contrary opinions in *The New Yorker* (under the heading: WHICH PAGE OF THE LUCE PAPERS D'YA BELIEVE?). So we in national affairs in this period were at times reduced, like Pascal's Jesuit, to telling the truth in a low key. And working to keep our own pages free from distortion. Alex hoped to hold our friendship while obliging Luce with a hard line. But my memory of those days is of trudging wearily up to the managing editor's office, asking him to take out heavy-handed phrases he had written in — such as referring to the State Department's "losing China," when I would protest that China was never the State Department's to win or lose. Alexander would eventually give way, a managing editor unable to get said in print what he wanted said; these exchanges were hard on us both and tested our friendship. I'm sure that such shadings were lost on most of our readers, since a few pages on they would find uninhibited polemics, but still it mattered totally to me that distinctions should be made in any section I was responsible for.

Perhaps because of this internal tension, for months *Time* did not put on its cover the mustachioed and newsworthy face of Secretary of State Acheson. Finally Acheson could no longer be avoided, and this led to the nastiest working lunch I ever ate at *Time.* There were four of us: Matthews, the editor, and Alexander, the managing editor, once friends but now hardly speaking to one another; myself, and Duncan Norton-Taylor, who was to write the cover story.

We set out for a hotel three blocks away, where we had hired a small private dining room to hash out the story line in advance. On the way I remember deliberately walking beside Dunc Taylor, rather than with either Matthews or Alexander, so as not to take sides beforehand. Taylor, perhaps Whittaker Chambers's closest friend and a Taft conservative in politics, had interviewed Acheson for the story and had found him haughty and offensive (Acheson could hardly be expected to love *Time*) but nonetheless wanted to write a fair appraisal of him. I wanted that too. Before drinks were served, Alexander announced, "If this cover story doesn't say that Acheson is the worst secretary of state in American history, we haven't any guts." It was all downhill from that point. Matthews and Alexander wrangled, Matthews attempting to be conciliatory, Alexander determined not to be. This unpleasant scene went on, uninterrupted except for the frequent appearance of one of those "Whogetza" waiters, crying out as he burst in from the kitchen, "Whogetza clams, whogetza soup?" After two hours of it, I said I'd never known us before to talk to death cover stories before they were written, so why do so now on a story so specially charged with emotion? In the end, Alexander absented himself from any responsibility for the story. When the cover story did appear, Geoffrey Crowther, the editor of *The Economist,* wrote Matthews from London that this was the fairest story he had read on Acheson. Perhaps it was — though I suspect it still reflected the fevered emotions of the times, and have no desire to reread it.

During this period, the idea of whether I wanted to continue at *Time* was sometimes at the end of the week a

55–45 decision in my mind. Was all this arguing worth it? Was it enough to be proud of your own section but not of the magazine? I tried not to make that assumption so dear to the liberal mind, that only his own motives are pure. The musk of ambition was indeed heavy over *Time;* there were men too eager to please Luce, but there were also men whose views though different from mine were as honestly held. What was remarkable about Harry Luce's *Time* was that at its worst moments, it always seemed to have the possibility of correcting course, and sometimes did. One would have felt it defaulting not to have kept up the struggle. That idea held me at *Time* more than did the simple inertia of a career.

Tactfully, when things quieted down, Alexander proposed that I trade jobs with the foreign editor, who after five years was bored with that assignment. It was a lateral move, but I went reluctantly, only to find myself soon caught up in the subject of foreign affairs, exhilarated by the freedom I was given and at my escape from the weekly hassles. I was therefore not the editor of national affairs a year later when Luce, in his determination to elect a Republican President after twenty years of Democratic rule, infuriated conservative readers (by the way *Time* denigrated Taft to put over Eisenhower), angered liberals (by *Time*'s rough treatment of Adlai Stevenson), antagonized readers who simply wanted the news fairly presented, and lost his editor, T. S. Matthews.

Manfred Gottfried, who had been the first editorial employee hired at *Time* back in 1923, used to predict consolingly that *Time* would straighten itself out once there was a Republican in the White House, for journalism always found itself at odds with whomever was President. It didn't turn out that neatly, but that is a later story, for with Eisenhower we inherited another one of Luce's favorites, John Foster Dulles.

Historians, picking their way through the shards of this period, have been rightly hard on *Time*'s performance. Sometimes exceptions are made; I have been described as a "house liberal," which suggests a favored, or tolerated, status I never had. If I sometimes gave trouble where others didn't, I expected to pay for my independence in periods of disfavor, which I sometimes went through. I regarded this as no profile in courage, but rather as the only way I could work there. I never thought of dissent as a work benefit: it had to be paid for.

Besides, I was not trying to put across a "New Deal slant" in the face of pressures to the contrary. I no longer wanted to be a washroom hero, to be judged by my colleagues on whether I passed all their litmus paper tests of liberal orthodoxy. I was finding such orthodoxy too confining an explanation of our times. My real quarrels occurred when *Time* failed to give the other side of an argument its proper weight, and left out evidence that was awkward to its case. That seemed to me a violation of the reader's trust.

Presumably we were all trying to find the meaning of events in the moments after they happened, which was demanding enough work. So long as this was the common intent, and everyone remained persuadable, each one's baggage of prior prejudices didn't matter so much. And this is how it mostly was. What I liked best at *Time* was the arguing out of positions, instead of the clinging to them. It didn't matter so much where you started in your thinking as where you wound up. My own reactions to issues had become less automatic. Once I had worried that ambition would temper my views, and had the young man's fears of the conservative corruption of age. I found instead that one had to fear more a rigidity in sticking to one's own preconceptions when they did not fit a reality. And that too is corruption.

The greatest gift of *Time* (and also the frustration of working there) lay in the feeling that it mattered, mattered painfully, what we said and how we said it. In that compression of the world's week, we agonized over the importance of people, policies and nations, seeking a relationship and a hierarchy of importance in events. In a way, it was overweening of us even to presume, but the nature of our task required an exercise of judgment in what we said or what we left out, a hundred times during a week. However modestly a Walter Cronkite signs off a news broadcast with "And that's the way it is," the assumption is immense.

8

AUDIENCES

1.

Much is made of the advertiser's influence in journalism, but I think too little is made of the reader's. What a reader is presumed to want has a lot to do with the kind of truth he gets, and how much of it.

News takes its final shape from an editor's hunch about a reader: What is he interested in, how long will he pay attention? How much does the reader already know about the subject: can we skip reading the minutes of the last meeting? Is he weary of the subject?

Observe how in one decade Africa rose and fell in news interest. It had been a continent called dark because of outsiders' unfamiliarity with it, peopled with wild beasts, Stanley and Dr. Livingstone, Tarzan, characters out of Conrad, and in the background, natives who were servants, slaves or savages. With the retreat of the European colonizers and the beginnings of new nations, subalterns from Aldershot became generals, socialists from the London School of Economics became presidents, men like Jomo Kenyatta, Nyerere, Nkrumah and Tom Mboya became real, and African blacks for the first time became individual. But the random terror of the Congo was followed by the sight of the gaunt ebony children of Biafra, and this in turn by unspeakable horrors in unpronounceable places, and though in other parts of independent Africa some kind of governing stability was being slowly won, the American public's readiness to sympathize, even its willingness to hear about Africa, diminished. Was it satiety, or a recognition of the insoluble? The quantity of misery and sorrow in Africa over the past decade may have been constant; the reader's willingness to hear about it was not.

For this the public is sometimes reproached, as if it were failing in its duty as world citizens. But even those good people determined to be "well-informed" about everything can weary of problems. At one point, when Cyprus, Suez, Rhodesia and Korea had ceased to be mere place names but had become a rollcall of crisis, Russell Baker suggested that the only way to get through the day's newspaper was to ask oneself firmly, "Is this crisis worth understanding?" I used to ask myself the same question when I was *Time*'s foreign editor, and concluded that every locality has its equivalent of the Arizona-California water pact — an issue vital to the area but boring to everyone else.

The binge of American interest in the rest of the world, not as lands to be a tourist in, but as nations whose fate was engaged with ours, ran from the end of World War II until the mid-sixties. It was a great time to be a foreign correspondent: his story was crisis, the excitement in his words was genuine, he brushed with danger and the front page awaited his story. The American preoccupation then with foreign affairs owed much to conceptions of national interest that have since been modified, from threats to our safety that have subsided, and from an evangelical enthusiasm that now seems romantic. I think the change came when the great powers concluded that their security did not depend on divvying up all the nations of the world into client states, subjected to their blackmail or their unpredictable behavior. The idealism of John Donne's "no man is an islande" sermon — translated into John F. Kennedy's willingness to share any burden, help any friend, deter any foe — was lilting rhetoric and widely applauded, but it sustained a continuation in distant commitments that the national interest could not justify. Diplomats like George Kennan believe that the American public oscillates wildly in foreign affairs from indifference and neglect to overwrought crusades, and to a degree he is right, but his own conviction that foreign policy should be left to the professionals, who might more sensibly get us into wars earlier and out sooner, is dream stuff in a democracy.

The conviction that events in Berlin or Rawalpindi had to be closely followed by us all, because our survival was involved, vanished long before Vietnam, which was itself a war that lingered on from a previous state of mind. A later generation will ask how a majority of Americans was persuaded that what mattered there was persistence in staying the course, rather than the humanity or value of what we were doing. That frame of mind closed many a mind. When *Life* magazine ran the horror photographs of My Lai, it was accused of printing them to bolster newsstand sales. Far from it. The editors published those pictures because they had to, and knowing that the reader reaction would be revulsion, and why-did-you-have-to-do-it? The time came when only so memorable a photograph as that of the girl hit by napalm, running naked and crying, could momentarily intrude upon a public determined not to think about Vietnam.

News is also what the public is prepared to turn its attention to.

2.

"You have no right to boo, if you haven't
worn the shoe."
Don Maynard, veteran wide receiver
of the New York Jets.

That part of any human being in which he is crowd or
audience is not his most engaging side. It is him as passive
receptor. He imagines himself as a loyal fan, who frequently
applauds and sometimes cheers. But mostly he sits, and with
bleacher wisdom criticizes plays he himself could not have
matched, triumphantly shouts out the correct answer that a
quiz contestant was too nervous to remember, enjoys the
discomfiture of politicians stopped by an awkward question.
Audiences are all those who are not taking chances, sitting
in judgment on those who are.

We are each of us at moments audiences, and therefore
subject to that worst form of arrogance, because unearned,
that is onlooker's superiority. Nothing produces more of
it than television, which the family sits around, as Churchill
said, like jurors in a box. Television trivializes subjects so
that millions feel superior to ideas they haven't really taken
the measure of because they got them in such oversimplified
form. It teaches us to bear the misfortunes of others lightly:
we don't have to look at it long; on to the commercial. It
rewards the glib, and makes hesitancy seem falsity. It makes
dreadful demands particularly on political figures, destroys
some of them and corrupts all of them ("In the minute re-
maining, will you quickly give us your ideas on tax re-
form?"). The inarticulate lose out, and the articulate
become wind-up caricatures of themselves, and having re-

quired such performances of our political figures, we despise them for it.

3.

An editor chooses his audience by the kind of magazine he invents. The last time an editor is a free spirit is the day he puts to press volume one, number one. Harold Ross, inventing *The New Yorker* magazine, made all sorts of decisions a committee would have questioned; was it right never to illustrate articles but to surround them with cartoons unrelated to them? Would readers resent having to wait to the end of a story to find out who wrote it? Ross may have had his reasons for what he did, or may merely have been whimsical, but years later his decisions could be reversed only after solemn conferences. By then the reader had a vote, and the editor could only guess how he would cast it.

Having chosen his audience, an editor becomes to an extent its prisoner. Some editors are willing, even servile prisoners. I knew one editor of a big city tabloid so determined to keep in tune with public taste that he narrowed his own interests — the hobbies he developed, the sports he followed, the books he read — so as never to be superior to his audience, a surrender of his own individuality that I found appalling.

That was never Luce's style, though on occasion he would send for all the best-selling books and phonograph records, and retire somewhere to subject himself to them all. You couldn't have paid me to wade through some of those drugstore novels, and I never remember Luce coming back with any profound conclusions (except to confirm his suspicion that our book reviewers were snobs). The impulse was uncharacteristic of Luce, whose way of editing was to be certain in his own mind of what *he* wanted to read.

It was more in the character of our rival, *Look* magazine, to take constant readership surveys and give the reader back, in exact doses, the amount of fashion, religion, and compassionate glimpses of the poor he was presumed to want. All publishers make such surveys, but most editors have only a sneaking curiosity about them, out of the instinctive perception that magazines must combine surprise and expectancy, and that what a reader will often like best is something he couldn't possibly have anticipated finding there.

When the relationship between editor and reader is healthy, the reader is saying, "I'll trust you to bring me what I want to read, and not too much of it. You know my prejudices. I'll let you move me along, but don't do it too fast." In such happy circumstances, the audience of a magazine is like the audience of a letter: to whom it is addressed determines its tone, its candor, its familiar assumptions of the other person's knowledge and interest. But when an audience is large, diffuse and invisible, editing becomes a matter of confident or desperate guessing about what will interest them out in manywhere.

I once knew a newspaper, a not very good one, where over the copy desk hung a large blow-up of a slatternly housewife, whom the editor wanted his deskmen to think of as Mrs. Average Reader: would she understand a reference; were the words plain enough? A book editor I knew had isolated his common reader, by computer no doubt: this reader was a Ford dealer in Wichita with a family of four, and his family "profile" was always in the editor's mind. All such postulations of a mass audience, I believe, lead to condescension in tone that any reader detects and resents. Mencken may have been right that nobody ever went broke underestimating the intelligence of the American public, but

I think the real distinction to be kept in mind about a reader is not his intelligence but his interest. Editors and politicians alike have often underrated in men they consider ignorant the capacity to make shrewd judgments once the complex in public affairs becomes a matter of concern to them.

It was an article of faith, in the days when I worked on *Time* magazine, that anything important enough could be made interesting to readers; there could be no such thing as an important *dull* story. Of course, you had to "get them into the tent first" as Whittaker Chambers used to say, by literary flair, and clarity in presentation might take a writer hours to achieve, but we never thought we were addressing a mass — and therefore stupid — audience.

Yet as *Time* went on, it departed from Luce's original concept of a magazine written as if by one man, and for one man, who would read it all. *Time* no longer counts on the dogged "cover to cover" reader; people choose to read in it what they will, according to their interest or prior knowledge, and some subjects — such as science and finance — have become too complicated to begin each time at the beginning. We used to argue at *Time* whether it was necessary to make debentures and deficit financing plain to an uncaring housewife who was probably going to skip the business section anyway.

Every field has its pretentious jargon, which can be avoided, and its insider's idiom, which can be explained. But it also has its unfamiliar terms which, to those who habitually use them, have their own precision and economy. To have always to define words like neutrino, meon or parity each time one uses them ("As every schoolboy knows" was *Time*'s favorite device) is to irritate those familiar with the subject without necessarily engaging the interest of others. Specialization and increased knowledge have taken us so far that the lexicographers of the great *Oxford English Diction-*

ary have lately abandoned their efforts to define all scientific terms in a manner comprehensible to the educated layman. They have reluctantly decided to use equations and symbols which can only be understood by specialists.

Music is a subject of wide interest but with an excluding world of symbols, and the combination used to trouble me when as a jack-of-all-trades senior editor at *Time* it fell to me to edit the music section. How intelligently can one write about a symphony for a reader one dares not confront with a bar of music? The result is apt to be an "enthusing" style of writing which I deplore, in which metaphor takes the place of exact citation; I winced when even so subtle a stylist as E. M. Forster was reminded of goblins and of the tramping of elephants' feet as he listened to Beethoven's Fifth. There is also a point in popularizing, which I am afraid is often crossed, at which the ratio of instruction in difficult areas gives way journalistically to side matters, so that a reader gets one paragraph of Einstein's theory to five about Einstein's beard, his violin playing and his political opinions.

Perhaps it is harmless to be fascinated with personalities in science, the arts and philosophy, and to believe that in this way one gets some dim comprehension of what they are up to. But there are times when the "well-informed reader," knowing only the idiosyncrasies of these distinguished personalities, may too easily dismiss what he cannot understand about their achievements. Would it be better not to know at all than to have inexact and diluted knowledge of important matters?

4.

By one of those redivisions of labor which occur so frequently in American commercial life, it is now agreed that television and newspapers shall speak to broad audiences, but that magazines can survive only by appealing to selective readerships. *Life* was the last of the general magazines. Specialized audiences used to be too costly to assemble, but the computer and special mailing lists now seek them out, and consumers through their credit cards leave a spoor of their interests that is easy to follow.

The reader is happier, and so is the advertiser. For, of course, magazines live and die not alone in their goodness or badness but in the efficiency with which they provide effective poster space for an advertiser, at a cost he cannot better, to reach the public he wants without paying for audiences he doesn't need. (The wretched hold of advertisers over editors is not so much that — as leftist critics used to say — they sought to influence the editor's opinion, though there has always been some of that, and some is too much. More to be feared than an advertiser's corrupting presence is his unconcerned absence.)

Specialized audiences are not necessarily superior ones. The phrase suggests an elite of scientists communicating difficult thoughts that only each other can understand. But to the advertiser, specialized audiences are more apt to mean a pride of sports fans, a nest of homemakers, or a clamor of hi-fi freaks. In fact, the concentration of interest that is most widespread is sex, and with it *Playboy* and its imitators hit the golden jackpot in magazine publishing. Their appeal was to what the Hollywood director of Marlene Dietrich movies, Josef von Sternberg, once called "the one bond that links all audiences — the animal in man."[1]

[1] To me, the real fascination of *Playboy*-style magazines is in the gap between the assured world of sex they present, and the anxious world of sex their readers give back. Their nudes are young, pretty and willing; therefore no one gets hurt (the infantile *Playboy* philosophy), and the male conqueror in his stereo-lined pad is a free-spending fantasy that draws advertisers.

The trend to selective audiences and to communities of interest in magazines is probably good and certainly inescapable. In reading, like anyone else, I seek my own interests: news, politics, literature, architecture, and avoid what is abstruse or alien in other fields. Nonetheless, I have misgivings about the journalism of partial views, for not only is information tailored to readers with special interests, but written to their prejudices. You know how a hunting magazine will feel about gun laws, an infantry journal about defense budgets, a girlie magazine about obscenity codes, a business magazine about capital gains. The result in the reader is to reinforce, rather than force him to reexamine, his views, and it's a cool customer who can resist the pleasure of having his prejudices massaged.

In the columns of special interest and service magazines you find specialists saying, "I'll deal only with the design aspects of it," or how to make money from it. They feel discharged from attempting a balanced and rounded treatment of the subject ("you can get that elsewhere"). A similar philosophy, or disavowal of philosophy, guides those magazines whose editorial position is to have none, but who actually peddle a wise-guy nihilism in which the reader is encouraged to trust no one and to follow his own whims — the morality of the beer maker who says you only go around once in life, so drink up. *Esquire* magazine's most characteristic feature is its "dubious achievement awards," which savage everyone in public life from no fixed view or stated standards of its own except a delight in put-downness, and the belief that if you're well-known, you're fair

---

But the letters columns speak of agonies of inadequacy, of homosexuality in prisons, of what-am-I-doing-wrong? Such letters alternate with puerile and suspect *macho* boasting of the kind that recalls the Marquis de Sade's contention that "any enjoyment is weakened when shared." The editors, having invented a voyeur's paradise, are shrewd enough to respond also to a reader's purgatory.

game. Sometimes the malice rates a smile when its targets match your dislikes, but more often the effect is forced, and in this playing to an easy cynicism, I often wonder what would happen if those who live by mockery would ever risk stating, to their mocking audiences, what they themselves seriously believe in. You know the answer already: a nudge in the ribs, and a question, "What's *he* so uptight about?" Though I suppose a serious reply would be, "That's not our business. You get your worries elsewhere, and your relief from us."

I come away from fashion monthlies and from investors' guides, from *Rolling Stone* and *Cosmopolitan,* each successful in its field and each cocooned in its own positional reasoning, wondering where in all of this do they feel any journalistic accountability to what is common to us all. And further wondering how much all of this marvelous selectivity, this fragmenting of audiences by tastes and interests, is in part responsible for our declining community as a people.

9

Memory Cell: LUCE

Bosses are men apart; you must start from there. They can be fair but strict, easy and gregarious, withdrawn or driving, or they can be all of these in varying moods. But a man who puts together a large and first-rate organization is not apt to be temperamentally at the matey, easy-to-get-along-with level. He would have gone bankrupt long before, or been smothered in sycophancy.

On my paper in Seattle the old general who was our publisher was autocratic and invisible; we were his troops, and he addressed himself only to his officers. It wasn't that way with Henry Robinson Luce. Here he was, in his aerie atop the Time and Life building in Rockefeller Center, presiding over a five-hundred-million-dollar-a-year business with all its attendant problems of printing, advertising and circulation, all the editorial exigencies of putting out such diverse magazines as *Time, Life* and *Fortune;* leading a constant black-tie social life with his wife, Clare Boothe Luce (who was always more of a celebrity than he, which seemed to give him satisfaction), a man frequently foraging around the world in his restless curiosity to see everything for himself and to meet everyone who mattered. I expected, when I went to work for *Time* magazine at the age of twenty-seven, that Luce would be a disembodied spirit never seen but much felt. Yet it was his own personal decision — having liked a ten-line item that I had written about Harold Stassen, and having asked who did it — that ended my tryout period and added me to the staff. And within short weeks of going to work for him, I, the newest recruit, was being subjected to his prodding questions, and put to the first of many tests. Time Incorporated was a large corporation, and properly hierarchical otherwise, but Luce made himself the exception. He could chat with anyone he liked in the company and this was not considered as going outside the chain of command.

In journalistic history I think he will be regarded as the great innovator of his time, for he did not so much start new magazines as create new forms — the newsmagazine; then *Fortune*, which was meant to "give industry a literature" and ended up being its most intelligent critic; *Life*, with its big pages bringing great news pictures, but also introducing to America the photo-essay narrative in pictures.[1] But what gave his magazines their dynamism was his own restless preoccupation with them; his instinct that you first had to fix a form, and then stray from it, improve upon it. And this meant constant attention.

[1] *Sports Illustrated* was an exception. Its origins were strictly commercial, which Luce felt obliged to dress up with Important Aims; not much interested in sports, he celebrated leisure as "Liberty Hall"; only after years of such elaborate pretentiousness and an antibleacher elitism was it freed to become a real sports magazine under the editorship of André Laguerre.

He had three ways of making himself felt with writers and editors. One was the memos he fired off each morning:

I think we have the painful duty of inquiring into the Chief of Staff of the U.S. Army, Joe Collins . . . When I met Joe Collins at a Life lunch he made a good impression on me. [But] in all our coverage of dozens of generals in World War II, no one around here had ever told me that Joe Collins was a superior man. No one ever said to me "There goes a future chief of staff."

All of this is not necessarily anything against Joe. There is no culpability in not being a genius or a great man. . . . But there *is* a question as to how far the Pentagon is infested with politics.

The Pentagon has a bad name throughout the country. It is a symbol of all the worst in bureaucracy, self-serving, fighting wars with cocktail parties, etc.

Maybe your reporters will come back with a ringing defense of the Pentagon as a bustling center of all that is heroic, sincere, patriotic and efficient in American life. I don't know. But it is your duty to ask the questions.

In general: how much politics in the army, and what kind of politics?

More frequently, the memos were an illegible line or two scrawled on the yellow legal pads that Luce, like Richard Nixon, favored. The most familiar was "Pls see me — HRL," often with a clipping pinned to it. Once I became an editor these yellow notes would sometimes descend in a flurry into my in-box. This was the Summons. Or the summons would come by phone: two impatient rings, repeated, meant that Luce himself was calling. Gruffly: "Meet me for coffee at the drugstore, huh? Five minutes?" "O.K., Harry."

And there, side by side on counter stools, we would sit, while Harry pulled from his jacket a pile of clippings ripped from that morning's *Times,* or if he had just been out of town, from a London paper or whatever he had found to read at a Montana airport the day before. Each was something he wanted to make a quick comment upon — suggest a story to pursue, a tack to take, a line to quote. I discovered early that if you had objections to make you should make them then and quickly, or he would expect to see in the magazine the point he had just made to you. Often he was proposing little *eye*-tems, giving the word a Calvin Coolidge-like country editor pronunciation: he was forever lecturing us that *Time* stories were growing too long, and he had a particular fascination with crime stories (and once seriously proposed that we should start a true-crime magazine). Some mornings he would be grouchy and brusque, and then his voice became even more nasal. He spoke in staccato bursts, and with an oral shorthand that we all soon learned to sprint along with: once a thought was registered he wanted to get on to something else.

More formal occasions were the lunches, which usually went on for more than two hours and could be a trial to the kidneys. One was the kind with outside guests — senators, prime ministers, university presidents, businessmen — along with writers and editors from our own magazines whose subjects were involved. These could be tedious but were often fascinating occasions, for they brought you up to date on events and also gave you a chance to appraise at close hand people who were in the news: the Shah, always intelligent but stiffly humorless; Hussein, a soft-voiced little man intense in his courage; Golda Meir, warm, motherly and shrewd — she could marshal her case with rationed skill, but had a habit of shying away from searching questions by launching into an emotional remembrance of the holocaust, leaving the question unanswered;[2] Bobby Kennedy, addressing all his remarks to

2 Once, talking to her one evening in her prime minister's office in Jerusalem, I made some remark about Arab losses. Her answer was as sharp as a proverb: if someone must weep, better his mother than yours.

Luce and acting as if the rest of us were serfs; Gene Mc-Carthy, the wittiest of candidates, but was he seriously a candidate?; Richard Nixon as candidate, self-consciously warning us that he had to say publicly some things which we should understand he didn't really mean that way (as if dishonesty admitted somehow established his honesty). English public men are much more skilled at witty and shocking candor in private. Some of our guests hoped to please by playing to our presumed prejudices; some turned out not to be as interesting as billed and did not survive the lunch. We were a hard audience to play to.

In later years, as Luce got more set in his ways, I'm sorry to say that we often got to hear less from our guests if he were present; the monologues we were accustomed to at our private lunches became intolerable when a guest could hardly get a word in. The only man I ever heard out-interrupt Luce was Reinhold Niebuhr: these two opinionated warriors, both fascinated with politics and theology but from differing starting points, were a match for one another.

At our own Friday lunches, with the top dozen or so of his editors from all the magazines, Luce might begin by saying, "I've got nothing on *my* mind," which was a relaxing signal that the conversation could be about anything. These were fun, for as Max Beerbohm remarked, "Good sense about trivialities is better than nonsense about things that matter." At other times, particularly in my first experiences around the table before Luce mellowed, he could subject some hapless editor to a long grilling in front of the silent rest of us. Or, enunciating policy, Luce might hold forth at length on such hobbyhorses of his as World Economic Policy, or World Peace Through Law, and had an annoying habit of emphasizing a point by banging on the tablecloth with a fork, or rapping the table with a gold ring he wore

94

on his little finger. When he got going like this he was hard to interrupt, for though he paused, he might not have completed a thought, and we all learned to make nimble interventions, hoping at an appropriate moment to break in like a child jumping rope. Any of us who could get him off a tedious subject was much admired around the table.

Best of all were his travelogues, when Luce was just back from a trip and would tell us, with relish and a keen eye for detail, about a call on the pope or a long talk with de Gaulle. He was good at describing awkward incidents involving himself, for he was not so much a humorless man as one who wanted to be serious when others might wish to be light (he never told, or seemed to understand, jokes, and anger might bring out of him a rare "sonovabitch" but there were no sexual expletives spoken around him).

There was one other way in which he kept close tabs on what his magazines were saying. On all of them, editors wrote "show Luce" to indicate that he should be sent stories which for a variety of reasons (policy, embarrassing references to his friends) might interest him. In this way, without having to read all of the hundreds of thousands of words in his magazines and books each week before they went to press, he could be heard on subjects that mattered to him.

In Richard Rovere's famous article on the American Establishment, Rovere spent a worried footnote wondering whether Luce belonged to the Establishment, and was right, I think, to conclude that Luce did not. Luce was a frequent dinner companion of the distinguished and successful, enjoyed their company and had friends among them, but retreated from any comradeship that might have impinged on his own freedom and independence as an editor. (If the news required that something unflattering be said about a friend of his, he would agree that it had to be said, but I've heard him add: "But wait till I'm out of town before you run it.")

Luce was a loner; a fundamentally private man. He made himself into a good, and sometimes forceful, speaker in spite of a conquered stammer and a tendency to ramble, but he was at his best in the give and take of two or three people. He needed his privacy to pursue his omnivorous reading and to work out his own thoughts.

He would get flashes of enthusiasm for men with sweeping historical theories, and once ordered boxed volumes of Arnold Toynbee's history sent to all his top editors to read. I think theological fine points, and the subtleties of political tactics, exhilarated him most. Though a Presbyterian, he got most pleasure from disputations with urbane Roman Catholic thinkers such as Father John Courtney Murray.[3] For a time in the 1940s he generally had a resident guru at the office to exchange profound thoughts with, of whom the least egregious was Whittaker Chambers. We working editors used to think that things would go better once a particular guru lost favor as each inevitably did; but soon there would be a new one. Though Luce might enjoy the morning's intellectual romp with such men, he never surrendered his thinking to them. Or to anybody else. He had convictions, but never let even the deepest of them go unexamined. His beliefs were the conventional ones — God, duty, country, capitalism — but he was too relentlessly curious a man to be conventionally conservative. He wrote this comment to an editor on a story in *Fortune:*

[3] There used to be frequent reports that Luce was about to become a Catholic convert like his wife, Clare Boothe Luce. Impossible, I would have thought. He sometimes went to Catholic services with her near their Connecticut home. He told me that he was aware of all eyes upon him as he walked up the aisle, and had developed a little stumble as he entered his pew, which if those around him wished to, they could interpret as a genuflection toward the altar.

The Allegheny Fight. This is a story I started out liking but ended up dissatisfied. I will try to tell you why. It has something to do with your statement about making money being the No. 1 motive. In this case I resent the fact that Kirby and the Murchisons are fighting for a huge chunk of the "national estate" (to use a phrase which Lippmann borrowed from, I think, Bagehot, years ago) — fighting about a lot of U.S. wealth without there seeming to be any point to the fight. Neither Kirby nor Murchison seem to stand for a damn thing. Kirby seems to be an utterly pointless man and I resent his having $300 million. Old Father Murchison had something — in the old Texas robber baron sense. But what about those two boys: if they stand for anything, Fortune didn't tell me. Yes, what we always want in some sort of sense, are heroes and villains. There doesn't seem to be any sort of villainy in this thing and certainly no heroism. The more I think of it, the more resentful I get. This is the kind of thing which turns one against capitalism. I resent having these great railroads owned by pointless men like these. And as for these vast investment trusts, I am inclined to think they should be abolished. Vast money-power without any sense of creative responsibility. So there!

Once when paper companies raised their prices for all that the traffic would bear, adding several million dollars to the cost of putting out his magazines, I heard Luce grouse: "You can make more money turning out blank paper than you can by having the wit to say something on it." In journalism, to him, pointlessness would be to mirror public taste without trying to raise it, to report facts without trying to understand events, or, having understood, not seeking to persuade others. All this required brains and courage, which should then — for he was a decided free enterpriser — be properly rewarded. He longed to own a newspaper, though he wondered whether he would dare throw out the astrology column as so much nonsense, whatever its popularity. He didn't have much respect for most American newspapers, having made a fortune out of their short-comings. "If newspapers are not doing their job for the Republic," he once said, "it is because they are concentrating too much on pleasing the public. Here is the sacred paradox of democracy. The people are to be served, not necessarily to be pleased." A noble sentiment, despite a tinge of father knows best.

On *Time* magazine's tenth anniversary, Luce declared that the magazine's originality lay not so much in brevity nor in organizing the news by departments; "the invention lay in that clumsy emphasis on the *instructive role* of journalism . . . causing a 'correlation of facts' to happen in people's heads." The job of journalism, he believed, was to "deconfuse the issues" and (he had a weakness for alliteration) "to foment and formulate."

You had to get people's attention first, and thus *Time* suffered from a curious schizophrenia. It was determinedly lively, brash and iconoclastic, and its cleverness could wound.[4] But Luce also thought that journalism should uplift, which often led his magazines into platitudinous exhortation. In his instructional mood, Luce did much to make science, medicine and religion proper subjects of journalistic inquiry which the popular press before him had largely ignored, and a generation of Americans learned

---

[4] It was less so in later years, after Wolcott Gibbs's devastating 1936 parody in *The New Yorker* produced some internal soul-searching. Shown a copy in advance, Luce protested to Harold Ross, who in a lengthy Dear Luce letter wrote:

> . . . I was astonished to realize the other night that you are apparently unconscious of the notorious reputation *Time* and *Fortune* have for crassness in description, for cruelty and scandal-mongering and insult. I say frankly, but really in a not unfriendly spirit, that you are in a hell of a position to ask anything. . . .
> Sincerely yours,
> Harold Wallace Ross
> "Small man . . . furious . . . mad . . . no taste."

about nature and ancient civilizations in memorable picture essays in *Life*. In his evangelical mood, he could be impatient and demanding of America. He himself ascribed this impulse to his missionary upbringing as a child in China:

I gained a too idealistic view of America . . . from the fact that the Americans I grew up with — all of them — were good people. . . . I had no experience of evil in terms of Americans. . . . Put along with the idea that America was a wonderful country, with opportunity and freedom and justice for all, and you get not only an idealistic but a romantic view — a profoundly false romantic view. I was never disillusioned with or by America, but I was, from my earliest manhood, dissatisfied with America. America was not being as great and as good as I knew she could be, as I believed with every nerve and fiber God Himself had intended her to be.

Greatness would come for America when it succeeded in creating "the first modern, technological, humane, prosperous and reverent civilization." But there was sometimes a zealous woolliness to me about Luce's thinking on these matters, and I did not share his romantic enthusiasm for great missions and great men. The lack might be mine: as a journalist I never felt much ambition to shake the world or felt it my duty to convert it; it was work enough merely to understand it. Luce's mind was a curious blend of *realpolitik* and high-mindedness: he was privately admiring of cunning leadership (as he conceded Franklin Roosevelt's to be) but often invoked the sententious language of duty and crusades. I was skeptical about world-saving projects, and leaned more to the British foreign office view, as described by Harold Nicolson, that "there are no solutions in foreign affairs, only adjustments." But I will concede that this modest aspiration may occur only to secondary powers, and was probably not how the English themselves felt at the height of their empire building.

Luce's belief in great men probably owed something to that childhood in warlord-ruled China, an experience which made him less fastidious about autocratic rulers in lands whose people had not yet risen to the democratic standards of, say, Cook County, Illinois. My own feelings were more like E. M. Forster's: "I distrust great men. They produce a desert of uniformity, and often a pool of blood too." My preference in public men ran more to someone like Jean Monnet, "Mr. Europe." Lucid, elegant and wise, he came at least once a year to our luncheon table. From him I learned two lessons in democratic leadership. The first is that when animosities and fears between two antagonists are deep-seated (as France and Germany's were) the impasse cannot be broken by trying to negotiate out their present relationship, which will only perpetuate the mistrust; they must be given a vision of a common future which is to their mutual advantage (compare that with the spirit of Versailles!). The second is that this vision must not be imposed upon them in detail by superplanners, but must involve from the beginning all elements in the community — businessmen, union leaders, parliamentarians and farmers. In ensuring the protection of their own interests, they will become advocates not enemies of the plan. Animated by such a subtle, sensible vision the Common Market came into being. I concede that Monnet's method makes less vivid journalistic copy than the roughshod solutions of "strong men."

Perhaps Luce was always more pragmatic than I about dictators — he apparently went through an earlier period of admiring Mussolini — in lands more benighted than ours; he was marked by Sun Yat Sen's paternalistic theory that great leaders must provide "tutelage" for their peoples until they are themselves ready for power. Among modern rulers Luce much admired Ataturk as a dictator who had prepared Turkey for democracy after him. Luce had similar hopes for Nasser.

One hot summer night in Cairo, Luce and I spent a long evening with Nasser in his palace. Nasser was at his attractive best, smiling and courteous and plausible: he was one of those men who at any given moment could persuade you that all his grievances are justified, and his own actions justified ("I only react"). Afterwards, back in our limousine, Luce as usual wanted to decide what was "the story" in what we had just heard. Luce was pleased to have extracted an acknowledgment from Nasser that Israel "existed" and was impressed by Nasser's willingness to be more conciliatory toward Israel if only Iraq or Syria would let him be. Since I thought Nasser appealing but shifty by nature, I said I'd be more persuaded once I heard such privately confided views expressed over Cairo radio. But after one such occasion, long before the Suez crisis, Luce wired home to his editors:

IN ANSWER TO SIMPLE QUESTION WHETHER I AM FOR OR AGAINST NASSER THE SIMPLE ANSWER IS I AM FOR HIM REPEAT FOR HIM. FURTHERMORE TO BE FOR NASSER IS NOT INCONSISTENT WITH PROPER AMERICAN COMMITMENT TO STATE OF ISRAEL. I FOUND TOTAL UNANIMITY ON TWO POINTS ABOUT THE MAN. FIRST HE IS HONEST SECOND HE HAS GREAT ABILITY. WHEN YOU FIND HONESTY IN AN OUTSTANDING LEADER IT IS SOMETHING TO BE PRIZED AND WHEN YOU FIND IT IN A VAST AREA OF PASSION SUSPICION AND INTRIGUE IT IS A TREASURE TO BE CULTIVATED. THIS IS NO GUARANTEE THAT NASSER WILL BE OUR FRIEND SIX MONTHS FROM NOW BUT IT IS ASSURANCE THAT STATESMANSHIP HAS REAL CHANCE MORE LATER REGARDS

LUCE

I enjoyed the clash of opinions with Luce, and they undoubtedly kept my views from being too placid. In five years as foreign editor of *Time,* during a turbulent period leading up to that catastrophic fortnight when Britain, France, Israel and Egypt were at war in the Middle East, and Soviet tanks were repressing a revolt in Hungary, I rarely had any serious disagreement on foreign affairs with Luce. (Only minor ones: I had constantly, for example, to resist his eagerness to accept uncritically the Greek side of the Cyprus issue, since he was under the spell of an emotional Greek ambassador friend, and was always susceptible to anyone patriotic enough to weep for his country.) But I could not be comfortable with what was then going on elsewhere in the magazine.

The notion that a Republican in the White House would restore our editorial independence proved not to be the case. The waspish Democratic national chairman of the day, in fact, described *Time* as the "house organ" of the Eisenhower regime.[5] Ike, however, was not applauded in the pages of *Time,* as I would applaud him now, for confident inertia — the military man's shrewd resistance to many mischievous opportunities to employ American forces abroad (he, for example, rejected suggestions by Vice-president Nixon and Admiral Radford for a carrier strike in Indochina at the time of Dienbienphu, which would have

[5] The relationship was indeed for a time close. After his election, Eisenhower asked Luce what job he would like. Luce replied that the only job he fancied was secretary of state, but didn't feel sufficiently qualified. In the end Eisenhower made Luce's wife ambassador to Italy. While she held the job, Luce spent more time in Rome than in New York. One incidental effect of this was that as foreign editor I had to immerse myself in the minute details of Italian politics more intensively than anyone but an Italian could wish to be. As usual, Luce discovered all kinds of ways in which the Italians might straighten themselves out, but finally concluded that they were incorrigible. Throughout, Clare was much more clear-eyed about the possibilities.

gotten us into the Vietnam war eight years earlier). Instead, if *Time* had a fault to find, it was that Ike was too timorous in implementing all the cold-war schemes of John Foster Dulles, who divided the world into good and evil and warned Nehru that neutralism was "immoral." Dulles, like Luce, was a Presbyterian, and as a public figure something of a creation of Luce's, for Luce had earlier allowed him many pages in *Life* to expound his views. Dulles was generally regarded as the nation's leading Presbyterian layman and perhaps the highest priced corporation lawyer in Wall Street, qualities which produced in Dulles an odious mixture, to me, of deviousness and piety.

Luce himself of course always favored what he called "a moral foreign policy" but recognized that "the peril of the moral attitude is that since you can't always be consistent in a moral policy, when you are inconsistent you are open to the charge of hypocrisy — and you make some people feel like 'throwing up.' " Luce himself was frequently torn by the promptings of conscience in conflict with his needs and opportunities. This might have proved too much of a strain for him were he not sometimes able, at the crucial moment, to disconnect his conscience momentarily, as one might a hearing aid. Once at a staff dinner he conceded that *Time*'s political coverage during a recent election had been biased, but defended it as "a little cheating" such as one does in bridge. I was shocked, even about the bridge part.

And so, though I was happy in my opportunities as foreign editor, left generally alone, and surrounded by a first-rate staff of correspondents in the field and of writers in New York, I was constantly troubled. Not long ago in the archives of Time Incorporated, where Luce had evidently filed it to be saved, there surfaced a long personal and confidential memo I had sent to him in February 1956:

Harry:

I write this memo reluctantly, and wish I didn't feel the need to. . . . It has gotten so no one says aloud any more what many feel. We are not asked; we have gotten the idea that it is none of our business, but it didn't used to be this way and I cannot believe that our present silence is healthy. I for one am no longer satisfied to do the best I can in my own area and wear blinders about the rest.

The plain fact is that National Affairs is not only bad in itself, it is hurting the rest of the magazine. It is dishonest, and its dishonesty is spreading a cynicism through the rest of the magazine. This cynicism, in this form, is a new thing in the halls of Time in my 12 years here. . . .

I have long thought that the Hearst empire lost its tremendous position when it failed to accommodate to the times. . . . Readers had other ways to find out the facts, and ceased to trust the Hearst papers. I regret to say that I think the present National Affairs section is now being edited under the same anachronistic assumptions that did so much damage to the Hearst press.

A good many of us have told ourselves that if the rest of the magazine behaves the reader will appreciate that, and perhaps we can postpone an evil day but I fear in the end this will not be enough. For National Affairs forfeits trust in the area most people can catch us out in. . . .

It cannot be news to you that National Affairs is as it is. But perhaps it is news to you that anyone on the staff feels strongly about it, and I speak out only because the silence of our convenience may have misled you.

Time used to "cheat" a little in the campaign's final month, and did so guiltily; now it's a four year proposition. . . .

I have heard your speech about Time not being a Public Utility. I know what you mean by the remark, but I have also seen and cheered the many times when you have regarded our magazines as a public trust. I know which of these two points of view I prefer, but I have no intention of trying to moralize to you. . . .

Though it was before my time, it is part of the legend, of the days when you and Wert and Norris and Matthews (and I do not know who else) had a great rassle over Time's soul; and you won by proclaiming that you would jeopardize Time's reputation at the point where you thought the National Interest was involved. It is of course not a very great extension to say at some point that the Republican Party interest is the National Interest (I am not saying this sardonically, and I trust in return you will not assume that my argument is just that of a Democratic egghead).

I do not think that Time is furthering its own interest, the Republican interest or the nation's interest by clumsily forfeiting its own right to trust. . . . I think that [Time] is in danger now. Not danger measured in advertising dollars, or immediately in circulation figures; but in danger of losing the esteem that you and I (and so many others on the staff whose opinion I cannot believe you are indifferent to) want Time to deserve and to have.

I am putting my case on the most practical grounds I know:

1) I do not think it is in our power to win elections; and our efforts (particularly our clumsy ones) hurt only us.

2) The many good things about the Eisenhower administration would be better celebrated if the reader could trust Time not to omit the bad.

3) National Affairs is dull and flat journalism, addressed to an intelligence and awareness lower than the rest of the magazine is, and therefore insulting to its audience.

4) Time has been hurt already among people who know better; it will not be long before others get the news.

5) We are getting into worse and worse habits; and like dope users, increasing the dosage.

6) By these practices, Time is endangering itself internally as well as endangering itself externally.

Griff

Looking at this memo sixteen years later — it wasn't the only one of its kind I wrote over the years, though probably more emphatic than most — I was relieved to discover that I had not in a private communication directed my attack at the national affairs editor, but at Luce himself. I remember thinking that, having made my argument as tough as I knew how, I must now be prepared, not just for Luce's displeasure, but for the possibility of being fired; or if unsatisfied with his response, forced into quitting.

Next morning I got the summons. Often one entered Luce's office to find him in shirt sleeves with his feet up on the desk. This time he had his suit jacket on and he stood when I entered, symbolizing, I suppose, that he regarded this as a solemn occasion. He said something about appreciating what my memo must have cost me to write; that he agreed that things had gone too far and I wasn't the only one objecting. He was going to change national affairs editors and I could judge for myself in the months to come whether the change was real. The change was in fact real, and though there were later lapses, and ones that I deplored, *Time's* entire coverage was never again so blatantly distorted. In these years *Newsweek,* with a staff whose top editors were mostly recruited from *Time,* first drew near to *Time* in popular respect, and for a while exceeded it; the advances in its own coverage, on a smaller budget, were impressive, but more important it was winning the battle of trust.

It fell to me unexpectedly to edit *Time* magazine in the next presidential election year, 1960. In August 1960 the managing editor suffered a serious cerebral incident (though within four months he made a complete recovery). As the newly appointed assistant managing editor of *Time,* I sat in instead. The magazine had begun to show troubling signs of election year Republican partisanship; I was determined that our coverage was going to be as fair to both sides as I could make it. There were office cynics who were sure that I'd soon have to get smart: I think they were right that in the old days such evenhandedness would not have been tolerated. My own attitude was that if Luce wanted partisanship, *he'd* have to raise the subject with me. Time Incorporated did proclaim itself for Nixon in 1960, but properly, on the editorial page of *Life*. The endorsement was somewhat lukewarm, for Luce had always liked Old Joe Kennedy as a tough scalawag, and admired his son Jack, whom he thought was anything but a liberal, and never did cotton too much to "Dick." I was for Kennedy, though not passionately, and certainly not for Nixon, but what mattered most to me was *Time's* good name in an election year, and in this concern I knew I would have the support of a man I was just beginning to know, Hedley Donovan of *Fortune*, whom Luce was grooming as his successor.

Surprisingly enough, the way to put out a "fair" *Time* in an election year had to be invented. The first week of my editorship all the stories came to me bland and salt-free, with Nixon and Kennedy getting equal space (as on many newspapers) whether or not each had equally made news. Louis Banks, the national affairs editor, and I agreed that this seemed too namby-pamby for *Time*. People would expect us to declare whether Nixon or Kennedy had won each televised debate. We would have to let the flow of the news take us where it would, even if this in some weeks led to a big advantage for one candidate. But since *Time* also had to overcome its past reputation, I decided that our fairness had to be explicit, and so made it my own business to see that in each week's issue the magazine touched four bases. In its coverage it had to record the best thing that might be said about the performance of either Nixon and Kennedy, and also the worst about each one, to assure the reader that we were not shading the news. I remember once when Nixon in one of his poor-cloth-coat moods was contrasting his humble origins with Kennedy's wealth; I added a footnote indicating that the vice-president of the United States was not exactly on relief, listing his salary, his expenses, his limousines and other perks of office. Another time, sensing an imbalance in Kennedy's favor, I footnoted a shoddy use by Kennedy of a 1937 Admiral Yarnell quote about Formosa, pointing out its irrelevance to any debate about Mainland China, since the Formosa the admiral was talking about had been in Japanese hands.

Time's coverage created a happy stir in the Kennedy camp, for Kennedy considered *Time* important because, as he said once, it went to "the kind of Republicans who could be reached by argument." Historian Arthur Schlesinger, Jr., working for Kennedy, was quoted: "This is the best *Time* political coverage since 1936, the best and the fairest." At least one Nixon supporter on the staff was certain that I intended a pro-Kennedy *Time,* but resisted my invitation to point out specific partiality.

As for Luce, he would drop by my office to talk over the campaign with all the delight he always got from politics, but he never made suggestions or wanted to see stories in advance, and only after the last issue before the election went to press did he call me to say how pleased he had been, and ordered me to send a message to the staff saying that the real winner of the election was *Time,* the Weekly Newsmagazine. A week later he told me with a grin that out in Arizona he had found *Time* magazine unexpectedly admired by Los Alamos scientific types, who wondered what had come over *Time.* "I don't know what you tell *your* friends," he said to me. "But I just tell them that it's the times that have changed."

And indeed (again with some regrettable lapses) they had changed, although in *Time*'s case this victory was not finally secured until Henry Grunwald became its managing editor in 1968. When Luce reached the age of sixty-five in 1964, he surrendered his prized title of editor in chief to Hedley Donovan. News correspondents from all over the world were summoned home to a big staff dinner at the New York Hilton. That day both Luce and Donovan seemed a little skittish. I was no longer with *Time* magazine, but was by then deputy to them both, in a job that was soon to be grandly but awkwardly titled Senior Staff Editor of all Time Incorporated publications. Luce and Donovan had separately written their speeches and had made no effort to learn in advance what the other would say. Fearing overlaps, or anything in one speech that the other should know about, I volunteered to read them both. The speeches were warm and affectionate. The only paragraph in either that I wanted the other to see was this from Donovan:

The vote of Time Inc. should never be considered to be in the pocket of any particular political leader or party. The vote of Time Inc. is an independent vote. Not an independent vote in the sense of some snooty or finicky disdain for political parties. And certainly not independent in the sense of any wishy-washy confusion as to what we believe. But independent in the sense that we are in no way beholden to any party, have no vested interest in any party.

I showed the paragraph to Harry. He read it and thanked me in the manner of a man who knew there would be a passage like that from Hedley Donovan.

Although formally surrendering his title, and spending more of his time in semiretirement in Phoenix, Luce was still heard in policy matters, and when he was in town he still sat, as the founding father, at the head of the table. But there was now a wry difference in his memos, such as this one sent to me in the summer of 1964:

> On page 27 of current Life, the Scranton letter is referred to as being "tactless." That surely is a rather silly word to use for a letter which everyone but Life seems to think was anywhere from deplorable to disgraceful.
>
> I leave it to your own sense of tact whether or not to call this detail to anyone else's attention.

Things did appear in the magazines that Luce had not seen and might not have liked. The kind of men Luce needed to run his enterprises would not have stayed, myself included, had they always fought only to lose.[6] His managing editors were strong-willed men and needed to be. The magazines reflected them, but were also clearly "Harry's magazines," and if this seems a paradox, the answer lay in what Donovan had called on that dinner night Luce's talent for "sharing authority without diluting it."

There have been various explanations of how the process worked. One of Luce's earliest managing editors once said to him: "Harry, I wish you wouldn't give us so much argument. Why don't you just give us a few orders?" Luce didn't; he knew he might order, but wanted to convince.

Television interviewer, to Luce: "I've heard it said that you think one of your major problems is to get good editors who will think for themselves and have independent opinions, without just trying to determine psychically what you would like. Is that true?" "Absolutely," Luce replied. "I like to see independent thinking. If it's going the wrong way I'll

[6] When Luce died, Alistair Cooke wrote in the *Guardian* that "the Luce staff was no longer a nest of skylarking college rebels but a palace guard of the American establishment, conservative, tough-minded, scholarly, unfooled." I think he got it about half right.

straighten them out fast enough." The answer has a Harry Truman ring to it, but it was also authentic Harry Luce.

More formally, Luce once defined the task at Time Incorporated as being to achieve "a consensus of opinion and conviction . . . and sometimes try to evoke it in the nation." At *Time* that consensus had to be formed and informed by individual consciences, "but we cannot evade the demand for a general coherence and a clear sense of responsibility," and this led to the editor in chief's unequal, deciding vote. In that formulation was all that made his magazines successful, and the source of all that could be agonizing about working there. He was too much the Calvinist to allow himself or anyone else to feel comfortable for long. He delighted in pitting man against man, just to keep things stirred up. Once Del Paine, *Fortune*'s managing editor, wryly remarked at an editorial meeting that the magazine's "editorial policy is made in a conspiracy between the writers and Henry R. Luce." The crack got back to Luce, and Paine was summoned. "What's this about conspiracy? You think I work behind your back?" "Of course you do," Paine replied. "It saves everybody a lot of time."

To work for Luce was to be in contention with him. "He welcomes argument so ardently," Hedley Donovan once said, "that it takes a certain amount of intellectual courage to agree with him when he is right, as is bound to happen from time to time." Luce was an intellectually quick-paced man who did not like to be bored and he had the rich man's rude habit of indicating it when he was. He was impatient with cant or with timid, calculated remarks; he liked a good discussion, but usually insisted unfairly on being both combatant and referee. He expected his editors to be "well-informed" and not just about the news of the day; to know in which House committee a bill was holed up and why; to register on all leading names in business, art, society, government; to know about the Arian heresy; he was also pleased if you responded to his own Corots and Segonzacs.[7]

The place was awhirl with opinions, some better than others; neither superficiality nor prejudice was escaped; and yet for all its dangers I preferred such a journalism to the skilled merchandising of passionless commentary, the lazy transmission of borrowed opinions, and the mindless exploitation of popular trends.

What may be hardest to convey was a submerged affection many of us developed for Luce. My friend T. S. Matthews, who has written of his own disenchantment, could also say, "Luce was not, I should say, what you would call a likable man; but there was, believe it or not, something lovable about him."

Inevitably it was awkward to work for him and at other times to socialize with him. At first, when early in my years at *Time* I was invited to dine alone with him, I resented this invasion of my private time, having already spent two or three long nights that week putting the magazine to press. Dinner was still work for me: a command performance, where you had to be on your toes, on your mettle and on your guard while eating the mediocre cooking that the rich inflict on themselves. But as the years went by and I came to know him better, I found those dinners no longer intimidating, and often left the danger zone realizing that it had been an enjoyable and memorable encounter. In his last years, with the maid having long since served dinner and gone, we would rattle around his big Fifth Avenue apartment across from the Metropolitan Museum till past

[7] Though Luce's own taste in art never advanced confidently beyond the impressionists, his editors — following their own tastes, or reporting trends — made millions familiar with the distortions of Picasso and the random imagination of the abstractionists. When Luce thought *Life* was getting out of touch with popular taste, he would sometimes request picture stories on such subjects as Sunday painting by doctors, a suggestion which would be unhappily pursued.

midnight, each of us renewing our drinks — my bourbon, his Scotch — and watering them at a bathroom tap. I don't think it easy to be friends between employer and employee. Sentiment can be the enemy of standards; if my work became unsuitable I had no social claims on him and wanted none. That was understood.

It was possible to spend an evening in his apartment, gallivanting lightly over many subjects or talking seriously about one, talking high statecraft or shop (in which he would be candid about your colleagues and expected the same from you); and then to be summoned next morning to be told of his disapproval of something you had written or passed. It was all business then, and if you could defend your course, fine. On leaving his office, I would then mumble, "Enjoyed the evening, Harry." "So did I."

On the last Saturday he was ever to spend in New York, he had invited my wife and me to dinner at his apartment, and then to the theatre. We set out late for the theatre in his rented limousine, and getting stuck in Broadway traffic, found ourselves talking, for longer than Luce usually devoted to such unintellectual topics, about a colleague who had had a pacemaker installed in his heart. Luce's curiosity soon exhausted my knowledge of the subject. We were late getting to the theatre, but the curtain was not yet up. It was a hit play, and on short notice, Harry's secretary had not been able to get the three of us seated together. The curtain had been delayed by some difficulty in the balcony. Harry walked down to the front of the orchestra, looked up, and saw two men holding upside down a man who had evidently had a seizure. When the ambulance siren sounded outside the theatre, Harry suggested to my wife that they both dash out to the foyer to watch the man being carried out. My wife didn't think they should leave their seats and said so; she thought the man entitled to his privacy at such a moment, and — well, wasn't this just like Harry's insatiable curiosity?

Some days later in Phoenix, Luce himself had a seizure, was rushed to the hospital, and died within hours. After his death all of us for the first time learned that one of his previous long stays in Arizona had not been a bout of pneumonia, as we had been told, but an earlier heart attack, which explained his excessive curiosity that night in the theatre: almost as if he had been watching in this stranger what he knew might happen to him.

Suddenly we no longer had Harry Luce's views to contend against, and many of us around the shop felt a particular void in our lives. It wasn't simply that a relationship that had begun in awe, fear or professional caution had ended in affection. In my own case I realized suddenly how much over the years my views had been sharpened, clarified or changed in combat with him; it was possible to think of this as a learning process on his part and on ours; I knew I would miss those exchanges, and do.

10

NUMBERS

On *Time* magazine, after our serious business was done, after we had decided whether an earthquake in Iran or a hurricane in the Sea of Japan rated mention and how much, we would sometimes, as we shared out a bottle of Old Crow, play a game of quantifying misfortune. Journalists too, like medical students, relax themselves with macabre speculations. And so we would argue: how many people have to be killed where to make news? Three people in an auto wreck in your own town? Ten people drowning in a shipwreck in the English channel; twenty-five in an avalanche in the Alps — and now the numbers increase sharply — one hundred in an earthquake in Turkey; three hundred in the collapse of a bridge in Bolivia; one thousand in a typhoon off Calcutta; fifteen hundred in a fire in some unheard of city in China? Try it yourself and discover how much your interest in any happening says something unsettling about people you subconsciously think are like you, and the rest of the world's many, who are masses, mere statistics.

"Names make news" is one of the banalities of our calling, but I think numbers more important. Statistics dominate our times, in a peculiarly exasperating way. They overwhelm our sports, so that no action exists for its own combination of grace and strength; before a forward pass completes its trajectory we have already been told how it affects the quarterback's percentage of completions and someone else's receptions. Success or failure, instantly registered mathematically, makes of sport a speeded-up version of our actual life, with its computers, polls, cost-benefit studies, market strategies and trend lines.

Numbers have become the dehumanizing characteristic of our times. They provide us with our conveniences and our cornucopia; their exactness, summoned up faster than the mind can work, guides a tumbling little canister across half a million miles to a safe landing on the moon; but numbers exact a Mephistophelian bargain from humanity. "Volume makes these prices possible," the merchant says, as he reduces his amenities and services, and runs you past a turnstile or a check-out counter. Air travel now requires such scale and volume that it no longer serves you, it processes you. The new rudeness also acts in the name of numerical efficiency; the customer, like the child, is told, "What if *everyone* acted that way? Can't you see how selfish you are being?"

The quantifiers are everywhere, prevailing over the romantics of every kind, the dreamers, the hunch-players, the seat-of-the-pants executives. What can't be quantified, for such people, can't be taken into account. Numbers give the surgical glove effect of something being scientifically considered, and those who think of people collectively are apt to regard all individualistic exceptions as unimportant, not relevant to the data. The supreme arrogance of quantifiers' fallacy, of finding reassurance in numbers on a chart however removed from reality, was Robert McNamara's body counts in Vietnam. He was only doing what comes naturally, a paragon of his trade — brusque with those who spoke of their own impressions, their hesitancies or their hunches; he wasn't interested in that.

Of course, not all business works in this way, but the race is to the quantifiers. Men who excel in such skills, our leaders of industry and sales, are not bad men, they are only uninteresting men, men of selective blindness, otherwise defined as concentration. I have listened often to them, at editorial lunches at *Time,* and for narrowness of outlook and underdeveloped personalities they can only be compared to the talk-alike jut-jaws who succeed one another on the Joint Chiefs of Staff.

What makes them efficiently valuable in business makes them poor counselors in public affairs, and I've never understood why their talents were considered so transferable; they have lived with figures that can be hectored into obedience; their hierarchical way of life has more in common with the military than with a democracy; as a class they are hostile to novelty, idiosyncrasy, or independence; and when forced to pay selfish court to human waywardness or obtuseness, consider their task, as J. M. Barrie's Victorian mother thought of the sex act, as disagreeable but necessary. Corporation executives carry their budgets and legal briefs home in their limousines at night, for they are driven to stay on top of what can only be assimilated by minute attention to details and to figures, in which they are gifted; they fly expensively to faraway vacation places but dare not spend much time there; they eat costly meals indifferently.

Harry Luce used to ask his editors why novelists didn't celebrate businessmen more, those who fought the epic battles of competition and made America's high standards of living possible. The earlier buccaneers of business might in fact have been interesting enough characters, but what is there to say about the next head of Continental Can?[1] He is respected chiefly by those executives who appreciate the skill and dedication of a fellow sufferer; he is envied most by those executives who would succeed him; he has power though not capricious power: it lasts only to the extent that his decisions continue to pay off on the bottom line. Quantifiers are servants of the goddess of numbers, who is a merciless deity. Their humanity is reined in by their necessities. Corporations could not prosper without their kind. But when their quantifications and charts and surveys fail them, when things take an unexpected turn, they seem not noble men who failed but practical men who miscalculated. They will live well in Florida retirement.

News too comes in numbers. And just as successful numbers in business consist either in their volume or in their scarcity, so journalists too find their richest treasures at either end of the numerical scale. Either in the exceptional, the unique, experience, or in what is shared in sufficient numbers to be common: if it applies to enough people it's news.

So much gets contaminated or coarsened when numbers matter. I am not suggesting that the popular will should be disregarded, particularly in politics; what disturbs is the amount of flattery and pandering to public prejudices that businessmen, advertisers, editors and politicians find it necessary or profitable to do. They act on the pretense of making the voter and the consumer feel a king, but they are not

---

[1] Businessmen characteristically describe as antibusiness those who don't accept their overevaluation of themselves. My attitude toward them in public affairs resembles Gladstone's opinion of Mayfair: "Looking over all the great achievements that have made the last half century illustrious, not one of them would have been effected if the opinions of the West End of London had prevailed.

really interested in his singularity, which makes him a nui-
sance, but only in what is herd in him. And this in turn has
produced a strange degradation of the democratic idea, that
of pride in the power of being average and many. I am ap-
palled by those who glory not in their individuality but in
the fact that their tastes being common makes them the final
arbiters of the reputations of floor waxes and comedians and
Presidents. The ideal Nielsen sample. Even the Supreme
Court, when it applies the yardstick of prevailing contemporary standards to define obscenity, suggests that if enough
people feel in a certain way, that makes it moral.

Quantification dehumanizes editors too. I have at times
found myself listening to someone's personal experience, unmoved until it struck me as representative and thus suggested a story. Found myself no longer thinking of right or
wrong, or of good and bad, as determinant of what is to be,
but weighing the likely success of a proposal more than its
merits, which belonged to a different category of reckoning,
that of opinion. This constant weighing of opinion, and
measuring the strength of it, is what makes the press miss a
certain explosive kind of story that it should have seen coming. Dormant inequality in American life isn't news; only
when it breaks out in impulsive anger, as it did in Watts,
does journalism — and the public — pay attention to what
it prefers to ignore. Behavior does require a critical mass to
make news, and much of journalism lives by anticipating
that critical moment when the rustle of a minority becomes
the stir of a majority. When it comes to making news, numbers validate any views, including Hitler's, giving them importance.

Once into the business of predicting the course of opinion, journalists turned to polls to make forecasting less of a
guessing game. They did so with ambivalent feelings. Many
of them secretly exult when polls go wrong, for polls have

reduced the prestige of those old-fashioned political pundits around every city room who assumed an intuitive gift at reading the public pulse but were often wrong, wronger than the polls. I find the success of opinion polls more disquieting than their occasional failures. For what does it say about independence of judgment, and each of us making up his mind in his own way, when in a nation of two hundred million people a pollster can so accurately measure public opinion by a sample, chosen randomly in areas that are defined by income, race and background, of a mere sixteen hundred Americans?

I trust polls least when they profess to record public reaction to such amorphous subjects as abortions, welfare or pollution. So much turns on the phrasing of questions, which then give a false authority to the numerically specific. The desire to count heads on subjects that are confused or as yet uncrystallized in the public mind stems, I believe, from journalism's competitive itch to be the first to proclaim what will soon happen. Such frenetic anticipation of the future is what makes much of journalism so boring, and explains why political races become so tiresome and elections anticlimactic. In the long succession of presidential primaries we don't judge a candidate so much by where he finished, as by whether he did better or less well than expected, for we had already been told how he was *supposed* to finish. The result of this preoccupation with the immediate future and what may happen is that the whole press often does worst by what in fact *did* happen.

In the end, opinion polls are useful as indicators but inadequate as guides to public sentiment. They make a dubious plebiscite, for views may be widely shared but weakly held. If a thousand people are visibly concerned, who is to define what the other ten thousand are not: are they opposed, apathetic, selfish, ignorant, indifferent, preoccupied?

And so if journalists are to judge whether any public issue is to be resolved or allowed to limp along, I believe they must still closely follow the interplay of three forces — paying mind to the zealous, the resistant and the indifferent.

So tell me not in mournful numbers.

11

PRESSURES

There is no such thing anywhere in the world as a state-controlled newspaper which can confidently be trusted to bring you all the news. And though there are state-sponsored radio and television networks of admirable integrity (most notably the BBC), they too exist only in countries where a free and independent press is firmly rooted, and where they benefit from that press's continuing monitoring of both their performance and their independence.

So democracy requires a privately owned press, and must live with its peculiarities. Among them is the inherent drive of any business enterprise to get bigger in order to outlast its rivals. But whereas in most industries the public interest may be most effectively served when two or three giants produce standard lines of bed sheets, radiators or ladders, such a uniformity and such concentration of strength is unhealthy in a press.

We seemed to be heading in that direction a few years back, toward something called Fused Media. Around *Time* and *Life,* I used to sit in on office meetings of that particularly vacuous kind where the uncertain future gets talked to death before it even hoves into sight. We spoke a great deal about what came to be known as the Thing on the Wall, or, as it is sometimes called, a Home Information Center. Based on the technology already in being, it was easy to foresee how cataclysmic the Thing might be: you could order a news broadcast taped in your absence so that you could play it when you got home later; you could summon up on the screen store catalogues, then press buttons to order and charge goods (what would that do to newspaper and magazine advertising?); you could pick *The Godfather* from half a dozen available movies and, by inserting your credit card into a slot, charge the added fee to your monthly bill like a long distance call; you could get your morning paper from a printout from the Thing. Was this where we were heading? And if so, would giants like RCA, CBS, Time-Life, Mc-Graw-Hill, Westinghouse, ITT and heaven knows who else be sitting down to a new high-stakes game? Fortunately the Thing seems an idea whose time has not yet come; the economics of it are even more daunting than the technology.[1]

Nonetheless, the idea of Fused Media has led me to question which journalistic habits and forms are inviolate and which are expendable. Must magazines always depend on presses, mail delivery and newsstand sales? The shrinking railroad schedules, the deterioration of postal services make

[1] Just how much does the purity and quality of network news coverage matter to the owners of the seventy-four million shares of RCA stock? That giant corporation makes radios, television sets, defense equipment, satellites, phonograph records, carpets, frozen foods; owns Hertz rental cars, a large real estate firm and Random House book publishers. If the point matters to that stockholder, not only are the NBC network and its five affiliated stations highly profitable, but network news itself makes money.

it harder to get magazines to their readers while their contents are still topical. I used to wonder whether *Life* magazine might better be turned into a ninety-minute Sunday night program, more intellectual and newsier than Ed Sullivan's, divided like a magazine into segments of hard news, entertainment, interviews, comment and criticism. Even better, reading might be matched to viewing, so that a printed guide in your hand told you what to look for in the filmed ballet scene you were about to watch. As for your daily paper, centrally printed, distributed by trucks and by a small army of delivery boys: would a home printout, if on not too sleazy paper, do just as well? In our society, things don't have to be *better,* they need only, like frozen orange juice, be handier.

That leads you on to thinking which forms of journalism have values unique to them, and would be a loss — society's loss — if they disappeared altogether. Merit may determine whether a particular newspaper or magazine survives against its own kind, but it may still lose out if the species itself becomes imperiled, as the hardiest of antelopes becomes no match for the most ordinary of lions. Competing forms of journalism are embedded within four industries — newspapers, magazines, radio and television. To those who work in it, journalism is heart's blood, but to its purveyors merely a part of the package and sometimes not the most important. Which form of journalism is to survive may be decided by quite other considerations: it isn't enough to build a better mouse trap if the mouse trap market is disappearing.

Government looks upon this competition with presumed detachment, yet if there indeed is a horse race going on among several forms of journalism, each vying for public favor and the advertiser's dollar, the race is oddly handicapped by the government itself, assigning unequal weights to each contender in no rational manner. Newspapers and magazines, long favored in postal rates, now find their rates sharply increased by the pay-your-own-way philosophy of the new postal service, which overrides a notion as old as our republic, that the dissemination of knowledge is a public good deserving of subsidy and support. Television and radio had the tremendous advantage of government assigned channels which cost their original owners nothing, and they got these without many reciprocal restrictions on the profits they could make from them. In Europe, where government regulations more strictly limit the number of commercials and the hours in which they may be broadcast, the viewer is bombarded with only a quarter as many commercials as in the United States. The damage in this country is usually measured solely in listener irritation, in his forced surrender to mood-breaking commercial interruptions in ways that European viewers would not put up with; it almost takes a presidential funeral to make station owners momentarily forgo their round-the-clock greed. But advertising saturation on television also diverts revenue that might otherwise have gone to newspapers and magazines. A manifestly unfair distribution of government favors thus affects the survivability of each form of journalism. Yet to even out these government advantages would require more intervention by the government than any journalist I know wants. (Even those editorial writers who advocate the placing of all forms of public transportation tidily under one government superagency — so that the competing claims of air, rail and highway travel could be sensibly considered together — want no such superagency laying its hands on journalism.)

I suspect that for the public, the question of competing forms seems too bound up in commercial rivalry. The public may think there's too much journalism around anyway, inundated as it is by repetitious accounts of the same few topical subjects, and smothered in information. And thus as so often happens in American life, matters of vital public concern are left without public debate to the arbitration of the marketplace, and to men who find the public interest at best an inconvenience, at worst an interference, in their money making.

Television, the Wealthy Eunuch

The most immediate medium ever invented is now largely a conduit for canned films, canned commercials, reruns, old movies and live sports. Networks have built their fortunes around government-granted exclusivity to the public air which they did not have to pay the government for; they relentlessly compete at the lowest common denominator in programming; they play the Washington lobby game for all it's worth; they are arrogant in their disdain for those who question how they fulfill their public obligations.

Television has left its mark on a generation raised in front of this seductive monster, this shifting parade of images and emotions, all separated by a demanding succession of commercial impulses that trivializes what precedes and what follows it — is it any wonder that a generation that has spent more hours before the television set than in school should be different — should be such amalgams of knowledge and cynicism, and have such little integrity of belief? Should seem united only in what it rejects and uplifted only by a succession of sensations? Television has raised a generation inexperienced and vicariously knowledgeable — the perfect audience.

Defending the lords of television comes hard for me. Only in their news operations do the networks contribute much to the well-being of the public, as opposed to its amusement and relaxation. But that contribution is a vital one, and its independence essential. Whatever one's own preferences may be among the networks' newscasters, they are as a corps men of competence and integrity. Most are seasoned journalists, and in addition have the special attributes of poise, quick articulation and pleasing public personalities — for the star system was the mutation required of journalism in adapting itself to this entertainment medium.[2]

Of all the ways to bring you the news, television is undeniably the best when at its best, that is, when its lenses are open on the actual. But its inadequacies have to be reckoned in, when more than half of all Americans say that they rely most on television for their news. For as Walter Cronkite says with characteristic freshness, this "55 percent of the public is inadequately informed. . . . We are charged with a responsibility which in all honesty and candor we cannot discharge. We do such a slick job that we have deluded the public into thinking they get all they need to know from us."

Television's costly news operation is run by capable and troubled men who know that more is asked of their medium than it can provide, since the visual is only the beginning of understanding. A crucial difficulty is that unlike print, where the eye can skip around, you cannot jump to the broadcaster's next item, so each item must interest everyone a little, and dare not go on long. News broadcasts have thus become an expensively produced, marginally informative

---

[2] From an NBC newspaper ad: "I don't want anyone but Jim Hartz to break the news to me. . . . These days, nothing could make the news easy to swallow. But when you're hearing about all the horrible things that are happening — there's something comfortable about Jim Hartz. You can tell he cares about it — but he gives it to you straight. When you see him calm and cool like that you feel it can't be all that bad. I guess to me he's the voice of sanity. And besides, I like his smile!"

news snippet service, efficient in what it does but in no way adequate to the complexity and richness of events. For any real interpretation, judgment and depth, you must go to newspapers, magazines and books.

A further handicap to television news coverage, against which its own journalists struggle helplessly, is its government decreed status as eunuch, the devil's bargain it made for commercial possession of sparse channels. In the opinion of Bill Monroe, a Washington correspondent of NBC News, "this country is already on the road, without realizing it, to a dual system of mass media: a printed press that is free but shrinking and an electronic press that is growing but unfree." He sees broadcasting enveloped in a "chill twilight" of government regulation and increased involvement, so that "journalism of vigor and independence comes harder for broadcasting than it once did; it increasingly requires acts of conscious courage." Or at least acts of determination. He quotes Fred Freed, an NBC News producer: "If you do something controversial you know you will spend months defending yourself to the government. . . . We are not part of the free press. We are licensed by government and required always to justify ourselves to a government agency. Anyone can complain about us, and a battery of network lawyers will be required just to keep us even."

Television's early days of Edward R. Murrow and Fred Friendly gave promise of a dramatic and lively education in public affairs. But no longer. Local stations often reject network documentaries offered to them — they can make more money by stitching commercials into old reruns — and do so secure in the knowledge that documentaries now draw smaller audiences. Howard K. Smith blames this audience decline on the government-imposed requirements of balance, which makes for dull and timid television. When required to balance unequal cases, all arguments tend to cancel each other out.[3] Smith looks enviously at British television, where documentary makers are free to marshal the strongest evidence they can for a case as they see it, as magazine writers do, and thus "arouse people to assent or dissent. Not only are issues clarified, but the programs are interesting and exciting to larger audiences than we get."

Testifying before Senator Ervin's subcommittee, Bill Monroe of NBC rejected the argument that "because the public owns the airwaves, therefore the government must police them and look over the shoulders of editors. This suggests that, because the public owns the airwaves, the public must be *denied* the most important benefits these air lines can bestow: information clear of government contamination. . . ."

I share Monroe's acidulous opinion that "the newspapers have played a shameful and shortsighted role in the past few decades" in being "complacent witnesses to the weakening of First Amendment rights for broadcasting." That newspaper attitude comes in part from the feeling that television, as the most financially successful form of journalism, depends for much of its reporting and many of its judgments on what it buys, borrows or absorbs from the others. Some of this is a stale quarrel; television has trained up its own capable commentators, and its cameramen, with their cumbersome equipment, have in war zones proved their own courage. In fact, the three networks have shown themselves fully as responsible as the printed press, and I believe should be equally free to set their own standard of fairness and balance, or else free to live in dangerous disregard of one. But this is not a majority view. And so broadcasting's eunuch status has become a habit of mind, which explains television's unimpressive record in forthright investigative

[3] No broadcaster wants to be so critical of the Ku Klux Klan that he will later be compelled to provide equal time to some Kleagle to sound his own Klaxon.

reporting of its own. I confess that I might have been less in favor of television's full freedom had its news gathering evolved differently — had any of the networks, falling into the hands of the highest bidder, permitted some right-wing zealot, answerable only to his own inexhaustible purse and to no regulation, to control and distort news. (Such distorting control by left-wing zealots would of course be just as obnoxious, but they rarely have inexhaustible purses.)

The justification for government-imposed balance in news coverage depends not on the dangerous power of the medium but on the scarcity of channels. Yet in most American cities newspapers are of one ownership, while four or five television channels and a dozen or more radio stations may be separately owned. Still, in other respects, television is a highly concentrated industry in which 87 percent of all stations are network affiliates, and networks provide about 85 percent of their prime-time programming. And the business is spectacularly profitable. In 1969, according to Brookings Institution figures, television's pre-tax profits represented a 70 percent return on tangible investment, compared to an average of about 20 percent for all manufacturing industries.

Only when this profitable oligopoly is broken up is television likely to lose its eunuch status. The technological capacity to provide as many channels as anyone could possibly want — through such means as cable television — already exists. Networks, for all of their complaints of being treated as eunuchs, have shown no keenness to hasten that day. With their astute sense of which crops grow best in the "vast wasteland," the networks resist the fragmenting of audiences which "narrowcasting" might bring. The public itself will certainly gain by the opening up of channels to minority enthusiasms, whether serious or special; to educational programming, to on-camera coverage of public meetings, and to performances that are unmarred by the constant intrusion of the pitchman. The gamble in such an opening up of channels is whether there would still exist large enough audiences for "free" (that is, advertiser-financed) television, which alone could provide the one hundred and fifty to two hundred and fifty million dollars a year that the networks are said to devote to news and public affairs.

Once there exist many channels and many voices, what need would there any longer be for government to monitor program content and presume to judge fairness and balance? The prospect of such a babel of viewpoints may be scary to some, but inescapable if you believe in First Amendment freedoms, and believe in the 1964 opinion of the Supreme Court "that there is a profound national commitment to the principle that debate on public issues should be uninhibited, robust and wide open, and that it may well include vehement, caustic and sometimes unpleasantly sharp attacks on government and public officials."

Newspapers, the Profitably Timid

The trouble with the newspaper business is that it is becoming more and more just a business.

The original owner of a newspaper probably opened up shop out of his impulse to be a journalist; the present owner more likely made a profitable investment. Increasingly, through a quirk in the tax laws, newspapers are parts of chains (more than a thousand of the 1,749 daily papers in the United States are chain-owned) and 97 percent of the newspaper managements are monopolies in their own cities. Only a few chain owners, such as Gannett and Knight, try to improve the papers they buy. The rest simply try to increase their profitability, and are like those hotel chains that take over great old independent hotels and prosper by efficiently stripping them of whatever amenities gave them character.[4] These newspapers become simple money-making machines; often though their physical plants are superb they are more frugal when it comes to news gathering; absentee management knows little about what goes on in the town and probably wouldn't want to disturb things if it did learn, and often has about as little commitment to the community as citizen as do the chain stores and supermarkets on the highway strip at the edge of town. Editors are chosen who will do their jobs without making waves. Such an approach is stultifying to good journalism, as anyone in a business knows who must deal with superiors who regard him as a source of expense rather than of revenue.

Only exceptional owners put their investment at constant risk out of a dedication to public service which many in their audience may even resent. Their numbers are few, and I suspect declining. Most of them — like the New York *Times* of the Sulzbergers, the Washington *Post* of the Grahams, the Los Angeles *Times* of the Chandlers — have long been held in family ownerships where proud tradition insists on sustaining the quality and reputation of the paper. Only from such pride comes the commitment, enterprise and patience to uncover Watergates. It is a condition that may change as the largest of these papers become public corporations traded on the stock exchange and thus more subject to scrutiny by directors who are skeptical of any practices that do not maximize earnings, and subject as well to the unsentimental desire of shareholders for immediate payouts. Corporate management may not intend to produce flabbier papers, but does so because a different morality — pure in its own rigidities — is at work.

[4] Many years ago, when *Time* magazine put Conrad Hilton on its cover, its reporters found him so delighted to see finnan haddie on the restaurant menu of a hotel that he was buying that he ordered it half a dozen times during the period that negotiations were going on. As soon as the hotel became a Hilton, finnan haddie was struck from the menu.

I remember once when the two oil-rich Murchison sons were luncheon guests at *Time* magazine. After their large operations had been endlessly discussed, I brought up their recent purchase of a respected but small New York book publishing firm. Now that it was theirs, I asked, what kind of books were these two rich Texans itching to put out? I saw them recoil at my suggestion that they would ever divert their hired publisher from making his business as profitable as possible. To put out books to their own whim or pleasure would be as unthinkable a business practice to them as losing money on finnan haddie was to Conrad Hilton. This helps to explain why capitalist owners cheerfully publish books whose political views offend them (Lenin once remarked that capitalism would sell the noose to hang itself) or books whose sexual explicitness would shock them if they ever read them. Profits in the marketplace are sufficient reason and sanction. One understands this in the making of curtains or shoelaces. Publishing too is a business, and ideologues such as Luce pride themselves on their commercial acumen, but profits are not their only guide. They will pass up money-making opportunities if their sense of propriety is offended, or will support unpopular causes if they feel so moved. The businessman is more apt to weigh such situations in terms of commercial advantage, concerned only if a profitable opportunity might compromise the company's reputation and thus its earnings. Guided by such indifference to any real values involved, publications often flourish better under corporate management than they had under a strong editor-publisher. Managers may sustain an editorial momentum without that strong editor-publisher, may even accept a certain amount of editorial agitation as a mysterious ingredient of doing business, but only to the extent that it continues successful at the box office. Corporate managers soon free themselves of editors they regard as negative, trouble-making, shrill or otherwise inconvenient. I am not convinced that journalism of vigor and courage can long exist without an animating independent, audacious spirit at the top that corporate management by its own nature does not produce and is never comfortable with. The commitment of the heart is not there.

And thus, between networks hobbled by government regulations and newspapers and magazines that are being rendered more cautious by economic considerations, I think the future of vigorous American journalism, as opposed to the journalism of play safe, is much more precarious, much more dependent on a few brave spirits, than is generally recognized.

Making Journalism Answerable

For many Americans, such independence is not all that desirable. The public thinks journalism too powerful, and its constant pleas of being threatened a whine. I am not a great believer in the immense power of the press, which I think much exaggerated. Most of the idiocies committed in print come from editors intoxicated by their own importance. Stephen Leacock once remarked that editorials would seem less formidable if the writer were required to sign his name *and address,* like a letter to the editor. An opinion is made no sounder by the power of a bull horn.

To me, the press is influential to the degree that the facts that it brings forth have power, and is least powerful when it is most polemical. Its power is in the light it brings, and this being so, the press must work at specificity; it forfeits influence when it merely rants, is lazy or capricious. An editor may seem a consequential person to someone who wants to attract his attention, as politicians and actresses do, but reputations once made take on an independence of their own, as Joe McCarthy, Jane Fonda and Spiro Agnew have proved. William Randolph Hearst in his day could decree that some names should not appear in his papers, and once in a moment of pique gave sportswriters acute problems by forbidding any reference in his papers to Stanford University — other teams played at "Palo Alto" against someone's "Cardinals." At a later day Harry Luce, choosing covers for *Life,* could only sigh and regret that Franklin Roosevelt, whom he disapproved of, was so photogenic.

I don't believe that bigness necessarily brings greater editorial influence. Instead the tendency is to become more self-restrained, more aware at any moment of "the enormity of the stakes" in what you do. In the initial, striving years of any publication, when the creative zest of the editor is most happily engaged, and readers are pleased with themselves for having discovered the publication, journalism is most apt to have the enthusiasm and vitality to take risks. But of course most consumers of journalism do not regard the power of the press giants in this way. Journalism now finds itself under attack not only from government but from a reforming spirit which has considerable public backing. The cry is to make journalism more *answerable,* and this wars with the need to keep it free.

The rulers of journalism foolishly treat their critics with undifferentiating hostility. Some critics, claiming to speak for minorities, assert a doctrine of open access to the press, which, like the fairness doctrine, assumes the right of all to be heard, and not just those who own the franchises or presses. This is one of those plausible but specious perversions of democracy like the quota system, which in the name of correcting abuses injects an impractical rigidity into affairs. For it ignores the rights of the audience to refuse to read. If by statute any and every element in a community is allowed to commandeer space to make its own argument, the result will be more than anyone can or cares to read. Judgment and selection are necessary, and other remedies must be found for those who quarrel with how it is done. To me, an editor should regard correction of error a duty; ensuring that all sides of any dispute are fairly heard, a moral obligation; and providing lengthy space to his critics, a matter of choice.

Still, those who dish it out should be prepared to take it, and I do not agree with those editors and publishers who fear the creation of a press council to sit in judgment on complaints against the press. The experience of such a council in Britain suggests that it would not be the threat to liberty that many publishers fear, nor as significant a force to change press behavior as its sponsors hope. Lord Devlin, who headed the British press council for five years, thinks that the merit of such a council is that "criticism of the press is no longer dependent for publicity on the hospitality of the press itself and the press has lost the self-satisfaction that monopoly induces." Lord Devlin, himself a judge, believes that "all professions have a discreditable past . . . their medical quacks, their rascally attorneys" and are the better for submitting to discipline. But he acknowledges that British press standards have improved less because of the influence of the press council than because over the years editors themselves have changed with the times and hold "as high a respect for standards of professional conduct as there is in any profession."

In the United States, I think the same to be true and do not share the alarms expressed by Arthur Ochs Sulzberger of the New York *Times,* whose opposition all but torpedoed the idea of a press council here. The *Times* refused to supply information or explanations to such a council on the grounds that the real threat to the free press is not journalism's own failures but government pressure. I don't see why Sulzberger wouldn't feel easier if journalism's misdeeds were dispassionately looked at, and proved not so bad as rumored (or if they are, they deserve airing). After all, a press council itself would not be exempt from criticism, and would have to establish its own trustworthiness.

From inside the craft of journalism also come assertions of the rights of reporters and other staff members to be consulted on editorial policy. In Europe, on such papers as *Le Figaro* of Paris, this claim has had more success than here. Most editors I know would prefer having to account to the known quirks of one boss than to await fractious committee decisions by their own employees. Yet I think any paper or magazine gains when its editor is sensitive to the opinions and judgments of those he trusts to report the news, and does not regard their desire to be listened to as presumption or insubordination. Whether institutionalizing such a consulting process would prove inhibiting to forceful journalism is the question.

The disquiet inside and outside the craft of journalism about its performance cannot be disregarded, and those who celebrate the advantages of robust free thought shouldn't mind a little buffeting. If it is to better itself, journalism should have the pressures of outsiders' dissatisfaction and insiders' informed criticism.

I believe that such crowding of editorial management must, however, always stop short of a veto, or of prior restraint on publication. The argument for a free press turns finally not on the superior wisdom of editors but on the need for ensuring a diversity of views. The difference between the political arguments heard around garages and those that the editor provides in print turns on an editor's responsibility for what he says or allows to be said. That responsibility on him cannot be averted and should not be diffused. Responsibility sits properly on those whose burden, pride and privilege it is to keep their enterprises alive, independent and healthy.

12

Memory Cell:
LIFE

I became the editor of *Life* magazine four years to the day
before it died. It was already in trouble, losing advertising
in clumps, as a sick man loses hair. In offering me the
editorship, Hedley Donovan warned that the odds might be
against the magazine's survival, but our goal should be to
put out as editorially good a magazine as possible, and if
Life couldn't last, let it be its circumstances and not its
editorial quality that was responsible.

We both thought *Life* should be saved. But we couldn't
be sure whether we were talking about a luxury liner that
was still queen of the seas, with a devoted following though
many others now preferred to fly the ocean instead; or
whether it was a stately but top-heavy galleon sure to go
down in stormy seas, its day long past. But it was a beautiful
ship and a good command.

It may be impossible now to wind back the reels of history and to recover the memory, in the days before television, of *Life* magazine's sensational debut. The moment was propitious in depression 1935: Dr. Erich Salomon's invention of the candid camera had brought new intimacy to the frozen postures of photo-journalism. Everyone likes pictures; the invention of the magazine would be to form them into a coherent story of the week's news. Originally it was to be called *Dime,* the Show-Book of the World, and its ambition would be "to see life, to eye-witness great events." And when the title of *Life* itself became available, for less than a hundred thousand dollars from a languishing humor magazine, everything was ready to go. On Wall Street the magazine was regarded as a gamble: its size was expensive and break-even costs would be high; the odds were so long on its advertising potential that rates were set modestly. The editors themselves were unsure of their audacious mission: they were trying to master the new language of pictures, which was then regarded as socially inferior to word-journalism. But from the beginning, the public took enthusiastically to *Life.* Newsstands quickly sold out. Editors had aimed for two hundred fifty thousand subscribers, but presses ran around the clock in those first hectic weeks to keep up with the demand. How big were *Life*'s potentialities? The publisher decided to flood the newsstands of one city, Worcester, Massachusetts, to find out, and sold an astonishing twelve thousand copies. Projected over the entire nation, that suggested a circulation of five or six million copies a week. *Life* was a wild success — and, stuck as it was for its first year with a guaranteed low advertising rate, a financial disaster.

Each issue was raw, original and inventive, lively, unpredictable and brassy. *Life* crashed the Party of the Week; showed How to Undress in Front of Your Husband, and achieved a dignified sensation with the Birth of the Baby.

Everything it did seemed as if done for the first time: its memorable candid pictures of the celebrated caught them off guard and humanized them; its patient, microscopic pictures discovered the beauty of magnified cells and stamens. And gradually Luce, the constant moralizer, found that "the photographer can make normal, decent, useful and pleasant behavior far more interesting than word-journalism usually does," and the critic Bernard De Voto noted approvingly that *Life* magazine, whose original formula included "equal parts of the decapitated Chinaman, the flogged Negro, the surgically exposed peritoneum, has decided to appeal to more normal and intelligent minds."

Life, with its success, gathered around itself a high-spirited staff, full of talent, cocksure of itself, and to those of us on *Time* magazine, riding the same elevators to a different floor, enviably glamorous. Starlets, not yet able to get nationwide attention on television talk shows, would do anything to get on the big cover of *Life,* and photographers in Hollywood would have had to be saints to forgo their opportunities, and some weren't. Studios would delay release of their films if *Life* would promise them a spread; Broadway musical producers assembled their casts in full costume for expensive "photo call" rehearsals in hopes of coverage. *Life*'s attention was just as important to major political figures, and to generals in wartime, who gave its photographers, artists and correspondents special status. Margaret Bourke-White witnessed the German shelling of Moscow from the rooftop of the American embassy, and Harry Hopkins was happy to be the courier who took her pictures back to New York. *Life* was king, and flung its money around as only a newly rich Arab king would. Even occasional attempts to economize were apologetic: there was *waste-waste,* which was to be deplored, but *useful-waste* was shooting one hundred frames instead of ten, if doing so produced one great picture. *Life* opened its checkbooks to get the best pictures, the biggest memoirs. Once when the *Saturday Evening Post* signed up the commander of the first submarine to journey beneath the North Pole, managing editor Ed Thompson gathered every reporter and photographer he could find or fly to England to throw a party for the entire submarine crew on its arrival there, and in one night of booze-fueled interviewing of everyone present, got the whole story before the *Post* could.

Oddly, though, as Robert T. Elson well documents in the *History of Time Inc.*, *Life*'s economics except for a few bonanza years were a constant worry to Luce and the publishers. They had, in its first runaway success, agreed to gamble a million to see *Life* break even or go to "an honorable grave." Luce was later to recall, "I once lost a trifling five million dollars on a wild-steer ride with a hot baby called *Life* and believe me, that was a lot more excitement than I ever got out of making money." *Life* magazine always went first class in its living, but rarely made a return on the investment comparable to the huge sums it brought in.

I don't offer a lament for *Life,* a defense or an apology, and I will leave to more disinterested witnesses the question of whether by other editorial means the magazine might have survived. In retrospect I think not. Its chief nourishment in its last years was advertising that was *forbidden* to television — hard liquor and tobacco. When both media competed on equal terms for large audiences, *Life* couldn't match television's reach or cost.

There was a further difficulty. In *Life*'s middle years its circulation had been force-fed, the consequences of the *Saturday Evening Post*'s fatal decision to try to wrest from *Life* its proud claim of being first in circulation, advertising and revenue — and of Luce's determination to stay number one. That war led to inflated circulations, to expensive bargain offers and to subscribers whose loyalty was transitory. Readers no longer stormed the newsstands, and showed high resistance to subscription offers of nine cents a copy of a magazine that cost fifty cents on the newsstands. The scramble to divide up the diminished market left over from television led first to the death of the *Post,* then of *Look,* at last of *Life.*[1] In its last years, *Life* tried to retreat to a more realistic circulation without signaling to Madison Avenue that it might be investing its advertising dollars in a terminal case. *Life* lost thirty million dollars in its final four years of valiant struggle to stay alive. It was time for it to go, a traumatic time for those who had spent their lives on it, a sad time for me, but what remains most in my memory is how much I learned there.

My first job on *Life* was to be its editor. But I had been considerably involved with it in the preceding four years as deputy to Luce and Hedley Donovan. Not just *Life's* economics but its editorial role was imperilled when television got there first and instantaneously with pictures — and with the immense added advantages of sound and motion. Maybe our still photographs were simply outmoded, but we also felt a discontent with the magazine's editorial balance. We would often ask one another what *Life's* mission now was (I found such discussions stultifying, and would answer a dissatisfied question with an unsatisfactory answer — that *Life* defined itself by being, as CBS does).

Though *Life's* first editor, John Shaw Billings, had early declared that *Life* isn't as good as it used to be "and never was," its earlier triumphs were held over us. Luce would recall a beautiful picture essay on autumn harvests, then suggest that the urban equivalent of harvest might be to live

---

[1] One of *Life's* distinguished alumni, Theodore H. White, has a different theory: *"Life* died for having rubbed America's nose too hard in the reality of the times."

a month with a modern urban family with two kids and show how and why each member liked the city. We poured the champagne into the same old glasses, but it seemed flatter now. After one dinner-evening of high-level worrying in 1966, Luce sent me a note next day:

"Somehow I think the *character* of Life is not as clear or consistent as it could usefully be. This is not to say that *Life* lacks character. It is variously impressive, dramatic and melodramatic. But there is a degree of uncertainty as to its 'values,' purposes, etc. This is partly because it is not explicitly 'functional.' And just to be a 'picture magazine' does not serve as it did years ago as a unifying principle."

With this I agreed, and two years later when I was made editor, hoped that I could do something about it. On all Time Incorporated magazines the tradition is deep that no one outranks the managing editor, who hires and fires, assigns and promotes, and puts each issue to press. Donovan attempted to create a duality of equal rank, working together: mine as editor was the more glorious title, the managing editor's (first George Hunt, then Ralph Graves) the more powerful role. Neither of us was to report to the other; each only to Donovan. I was to be responsible for long-range thinking about the magazine as well as for critical analysis of its present performance, in "tone, emphasis, policy and standards." I was thus not so much copilot as navigator. The arrangement required a congenial partnership with the managing editor, in which I was lucky.

Some of *Life*'s first great generation of photographers were still around — Alfred Eisenstaedt, dapper, meticulous and persistent; Dmitri Kessel, who captured the beauty of great cathedrals and lived with generous gusto; Gjon Mili, an Albanian of warm sentiment and purity of feeling, in whom, as with Jim Agee, a mountaineer's integrity underlay his sophistication. There were such later stars as Mark Kauffman, John Dominis and David Douglas Duncan, and a fine new generation including Larry Burrows (who was to die in Vietnam), Co Rentmeester, Bill Eppridge and John Loengard. On *Time* we had somewhat disdained the glamor and flamboyance of *Life* photographers, who seemed always to be dashing off in Mercedes Benzes with beautiful models in tow, or returning from abroad with more rare rugs or new paintings to stash in Kansas City warehouses. (Eliot Elisofon, on being told by his reporter companion on an overseas assignment, "Eliot, you've got to stop telling everyone we meet that you're the world's greatest photographer": "Okay, from now on you tell them.") On my old paper in Seattle we thought any available photographer capable of doing whatever came up. On *Life,* I frequently saw the picture editor refuse to assign a story if he couldn't get the right photographer for it, and got some dim recognition of how one photographer's solemn patience and creativity produced memorable somber picture essays like W. Eugene Smith's Spanish village; how Gjon Mili would carefully dissect a dancer's movements or a runner's stride to know best how to arrest in one stopped instant its purest form, how others would study a man's countenance and gestures in order to elicit from him that moment most revealing of character. What was most prized in *Life* photographers was neither technique nor a talent for lucky accidents, but the ability to enter an unfamiliar situation, size it up as a story as a good writer would, and with the mind's eye conceive what sequences of action, what angles of vision were necessary to show wordlessly how a doctor operates, a soldier fights and relaxes, a mother protects.

On *Life,* editors too thought first in pictorial elements, and if they found none in a situation, their curiosity fell off. On *Time,* we had carefully followed legislatures, watched the interplay of markets and prices, studied diplomatic maneuvers. Temperaments on the two magazines were different too: *Life*'s enthusiastic, where *Time* encouraged skepticism; headlong, where *Time* made comparisons. I liked the people of *Life* — the energetic gaiety of Mary Leatherbee, the passion of Phil Kunhardt, the moral impatience of Loudon Wainwright — but marveled at how important issues in public affairs were of natural consuming interest to no more than half a dozen staff members. On *Life*, strong views in politics did not require close knowledge. News gave *Life* its urgency, but it pursued only what interested it, what lent itself best to pictures, what its editors cared most deeply about. All else it left to the car radio and to the back pages of the daily paper. *Time* magazine constantly asked of something what its significance was; *Life* preferred to ask, what's it like? This was to arrive at understanding by another route, and when I came to respect both approaches, I realized that *Time* was more about meaning, *Life* about feeling.

At *Life* I was to discover, as John Stuart Mill had long ago, the intellectual importance of feelings. Not that I could claim in myself to be, like Mill, a well-tuned reasoning machine. Mill's father, to whom display was abhorrent and any intensity in feeling deplorable, had fed his son with Greek from the age of three, Latin at eight, algebra and calculus before twelve; and this lad, so crammed with knowledge and starved of imagination, had undergone a mental crisis at the age of twenty. Poor Mill, discovering later in the love of his life, Harriet, someone who could *feel* and therefore ennobling hers as the "perfect mind," became convinced that one must consider "Feeling at least as valuable as Thought, & Poetry not only on a par with, but the necessary condition of, any true and comprehensive Philosophy." There is something endearingly naïve about Mill's autobiography, yet he could also observe that "what made Wordsworth's poems a medicine for my state of mind was that they expressed, not mere outward beauty, but states of feeling, and of thought colored by feeling, under the excitement of beauty."

It was precisely such "thought colored by feeling, under the excitement of beauty" that I was to discover in the best of *Life's* photography and writing. It was not the beauty of mere prettiness, but of exact and loving rendering of wounded and exhausted soldiers, or of haunting slum children in the hillside tin hovels of a Brazilian *favela.*

Feeling gave *Life* much of its vitality, but when all its gifted young reporters were encouraged (in the mercifully fleeting phrase of that day) "to do his own thing," their fascination with the hates and passions of the flower generation was hard to distinguish from endorsement, and *Life* articles occasionally seemed to suggest that a little body-grappling between strangers was just the right therapy for all us uptight people. I felt about some of the magazine's enthusiasms like the critic who wrote of Sarah Bernhardt: "She awakened the senses and sent the intellect to sleep."

Yet I also sympathized with writers who chafed under the need to conform in their articles to company policy on all important matters, and felt that unless this attitude changed we could no longer hope to hold the best writers. I liked a variety of voices in the magazine, though recognizing that in such a cacophony of views, the clarity of *Life's* own signal would diminish. So I wanted to revive our editorial page, freed of some of the ponderous moralizing it was sometimes guilty of, making editorials short, lively and about subjects that we otherwise scamped. We were jauntily up to date on the heartfelt maunderings of the latest rock star and his incoherent complaints about society, but often neglected to introduce to our readers important people in government, in business, in science and art. There was a dread of talking seriously about serious subjects; this awakened staff memories of turgid articles *Life* used to run by John Foster Dulles, and of what one editor called "the dead hand of high purpose." Being in deep trouble, *Life* daren't be "too heavy." I wasn't for overlaying everything with dollops of portentousness either, but thought that in pursuit of the highly readable, we often underestimated public interest in the economy and in public affairs. I never thought that eight million subscribers in a nation of two hundred million made *Life* a "mass magazine."[2] Like Luce, I thought that people wanted their minds stretched a little.

At our sharp and lively editors' lunches, where over the martinis everyone had his chance to filibuster for his own enthusiasms, we sometimes achieved our balances with my weight at one end of the seesaw.

Bigness gave us the chance to command the best, and to deploy our writers and photographers as no newspaper or magazine could. But bigness could immobilize too; we could respond quickly, but only slowly change. I came to see why some intellectual friends of mine preferred *Life* to *Time:* the universal appeal of pictures, like the companion arts of slapstick and pantomime, speak of things plain to all while touching the subconscious at levels which the discriminating can enjoy. This universality of appeal gave us the burden of being a "family magazine." At a time when other magazines were setting newsstand records with the discovery of the marketability of pubic hair, *Life* would hear from indignant parents did we but expose too much white expanse of Sophia Loren's well-tethered breasts. How could you edit only to what fourteen-year-old daughters must be shielded from? To me, the answer was to be more reserved in pictures than

[2] Television's news programs have widest appeal to the lowest edge of the mass audience in education and income. People who *read* at all are already a cut above mass.

in words, and if we were, our words could be suitably adult. We thus praised movies that were more visually explicit than we dared be, and acclaimed novels whose four-letter words we would not use. We could still be adult in how we judged them.

"Family magazine," and the Luce tradition, gave us obligations to respectability too, and seemed to invite moral advice. I remember an important automobile advertiser, tough and aggressive in the Detroit way and Roman Catholic in his moral certainties, asking me: "Why doesn't *Life* take the moral leadership in our country?" His question was flattering in a way, though it assumed that *Life* could be didactically certain in its moral instruction when all other forms of contemporary authority, including the church, were perplexed.

I replied that *Life* was most persuasive when its moral values were implicit in the particular and specific — in searching out corruption, in raising alarms about neglect, in finding causes worth fighting for, or qualities of living worth celebrating. This wasn't quite what he meant. He was a decent, concerned man, but struck me as the kind who submits himself to Sunday sermons secure in the belief that others are more in need of them than he. In this he seemed to me to reflect the times, which were full of moral passion, but most of it expended on disapproving someone else's conduct: the young thinking their elders indifferent or complacent toward the less favored; older people thinking the young too heedless in their scorn of hard-won achievements. And here, without too overt moralizing, I thought *Life* could span the gulf, for we had shaped our magazine into one that made an authentic appeal to many audiences, and this shared experience made ours the last large-scale reading audience assembled each week in America. *Life* occupied a place where the Detroit executive might find some of his own views and prejudices echoed but others of them disturbed, and where the concerns of his college age sons were not dismissed out of hand, for the magazine spoke to them too (in fact, most of our audience was from eighteen to thirty-four years old).

But Madison Avenue, pursuing its own interests, didn't value such diversity, and demanded better-targeted audiences for its products.[3] I sometimes thought of that automobile executive when thumbing through the ad-fattened pages of *Playboy*. Those who preside over America's most respected corporations are almost to a man upright, Republican, conservative, alarmed by a collapse of values in American life, disturbed about their children. They put their advertising dollars in *Playboy*, and after business hours cluck about a national decline in moral standards.

But was the idea of a general audience magazine like *Life* anachronistic? In making the argument for it was I simply starting from the case I was stuck with? As *Life*'s fortunes continued to fall, in the magazine's last months I made a proposal that would not change our appearance or contents significantly, but our outlook dramatically. Why not abandon our ambitious attempt to bridge generations and simply edit for that majority of our readers who were under thirty-five? I didn't propose to be gimmicky about it: if anyone over thirty-five felt his own interests reflected in *Life*, fine. But we would be instantly freed of that awkward need to translate to different audiences — to wonder if oldsters needed to be introduced to the Grateful Dead or whether the young would understand a Korean War ref-

---

[3] *Life*'s readership was assumed to be roughly half male, half female. Advertising for most products sold in supermarkets and drugstores is addressed to women, and to isolate *Life*'s women readers only made the magazine too expensive. They could be reached in women's magazines at about two-thirds the cost of *Life,* and on daytime TV for about *half* what *Life* charged.

erence — those common-denominator considerations that took untold life and flavor out of our writing and editing. If it was true, as I thought it was, that people under thirty-five — whether conservative, liberal or politically indifferent — saw society with a fundamentally different perspective; that much about what they were groping for was right in its dissatisfaction and unsure but open in its direction, we would be able to make the change in good conscience, and would find it invigorating. It wasn't necessary to go youth-mongering, flattering youth's every passing enthusiasm, or to use trendy, wow, with-it expressions. Much of our staff was young and sympathetic to such currents; some of us in top positions might have to get out of the way sooner, but *Life* would find itself more out front rather than, as it so often was, coming up from behind, explaining.

The idea was never seriously examined. Management was mindful of how disastrous it had been to promote a *new Saturday Evening Post,* which lost old readers without attracting new ones. Was this again generals fighting the last war? Economic questions — such as whether to reduce *Life*'s large page size or to publish fortnightly instead of weekly — were endlessly studied and as frequently rejected. Any basic change in the magazine's audience appeal was stoically not considered.

Television had not only taken *Life*'s wallet, it had stolen its act, and was now where all the ambitious most wanted to be seen, and where the biggest news stories were pictured first. Wobbling around trying to redefine itself, *Life* for a time had all but abandoned spot news to television and wandered off into ancient civilizations and nature studies. These could be first-rate, but a vitality was missing. I thought *Life*'s first duty was to make vivid our own times. The presence of news, I thought, had to be strongly felt in *Life,* but treated differently. We lavished our longest hours, our latest nights, our costliest postponements of deadlines on *events* — presidential trips or cyclones in Pakistan — yet often the latest news photo we hurried to the printers was the most dated thing in the magazine that reached its readers by erratic mail the following week. On stories which television had been all over, and radio had repeated hourly on the hour and newspapers given all the details of, I thought we should cease indicating the enormity of the event by the number of pages given over to it. We should still assign people to cover these saturated events, but if their words and pictures added nothing new, we should ruthlessly skip them. In the end, Phil Kunhardt and Bob Ajemian devised the Beat of Life as a means to open the magazine with large dramatic news pictures and a minimum of accompanying words. Great still pictures do stop the action and fix it in your mind, and I believe that most people's recall of Vietnam owes more to Larry Burrows's photographs than to endless reels of television film.

A second kind of news I thought of as *news in the air,* topical subjects on people's minds but with a cycle of interest of perhaps a month or two. On these we didn't have to follow self-consciously after television but could bring our own inventiveness into play. Besides these two kinds of news, both external to the reader, there existed a third news domain. Once, complaining how difficult it was for a contemporary novelist to outdo journalism, Saul Bellow remarked, "News, *word of itself,* is what the public wants." I thought the changing human condition a rich field for *Life* to concentrate upon — the besieged family, the alienation and confusion of youth, the disintegration of old values and the inadequacies of the new ones, the new sexual freedoms and the disturbed results, the uprootedness of an older generation which found itself also liberated from what it once felt required to put up with. We would be missing the mother lode if we soberly pursued such subjects only as problems; people now saw in the lives of others not just glimpses of exotic or alien worlds but clues to ways of living for themselves.

This well-traversed domain was, of course, also crisscrossed by women's magazines and television cameras, for all forms of journalism tend to converge, imitating each other's most successful techniques and unabashedly scavenging subjects from one another. It was no longer enough to have done such things first: freshness consisted in constantly freeing yourself from what you and others were doing too similarly in the present. *Life*'s skill was to provide an understanding of a general condition not by statistics but by a close study of the particular, seeking out people whose lives exemplified a situation and had no distorting circumstance that would make them unrepresentative of it. A reporter and photographer would then spend weeks living with them, and having selected someone because he was representative, would find in him what was quirkily singular, individual and human. The contrariness, the unexpected resilience and candor of people, only slowly unfolds with trust. There have been many quickie imitations of this method, and much faking of it, but really revealing studies like ours took time, sympathy and care.

The pursuit of these three kinds of news was not in dispute among my colleagues; was in fact familiar ground and their own inclination; my concern was to structure an emphasis on these things we did best, avoiding the marginal and routine. In the final eighteen months of *Life*'s existence, I think all its top editors felt that we had put together a working combination. The menu was about right; what mattered was what came out of the kitchen.

Alas, we were no longer able to produce a magazine

with the luxurious abandon of old, when *Life* people had been the biggest check-grabbers in the business. Just one year before *Life* ceased publication, the size of the staff was severely reduced, and so was the budget for color. Fewer photographers and reporters meant less time spent on assignments, and though some of this had been excessive and was well-ended, stories were now pursued only if they seemed sure to reach print, though the best stories often begin as the riskiest gambles. The margin for discarding — so crucial to good editing — got thinner and thinner. Abroad and at home the closing of news bureaus shortened our antennae so that more story ideas had to be generated in New York. *Life's* prize investigating squad, whose reporting had undone a Supreme Court justice, unseated at least two senators, a congressman and a governor, had to be abandoned as too costly. Often sued for libel, it had never lost a suit in court, though each investigative article cost *Life* about fifty thousand dollars in legal fees to ward off suits which were filed and later dropped.

What once we did opulently we now did parsimoniously. Most other magazine editors, who didn't have our expensive overhead, might have envied us an editorial budget that even with all the cutbacks still ran to about ten million dollars a year. Such is the mad disproportion of spending these days, however, that the three television networks spent almost as much in one night to bring the public the un-suspenseful news of Nixon's landslide over McGovern than all of *Life's* editorial expenses for a year. And my pleasure in watching the football Superbowl was lessened by my awareness that the money spent on commercials during these three premium hours would have paid our editorial costs all year.

In *Life's* final days I thought our reduced staff was still gamely capable of coverage to be proud of. Enthusiasm was still high, though less carefree, among *Life's* spirited veterans and fresh young journalists, and going to press each week was a happy tumult. But I feared that we were not producing *enough* magazine, and might not be able to sustain its quality level much longer. The skimpiness of advertising pages was dispiriting, not only to us, but to those who remembered the lavish thickness of the earlier *Life.* In October and November 1972, when other magazines began to gain advertising pages in a business upturn but we did not, management which had carried a losing *Life* so long could no longer justify its losses. When the marketplace makes its final judgment, there is no higher court of appeal. Ralph Graves, the managing editor, in telling a stunned staff the news of *Life's* closing predicted that most of them would find other jobs (as they did) but would not probably again share such satisfaction as they had known together in putting out *Life.* It was a proud defiant note to end on, and characteristic of *Life.*

After *Life's* death, management discovered how much the magazine was missed, as evidenced in the readiness of hundreds of thousands of readers to pay twenty dollars for a book of *The Best of Life* photographs. Its circulation, its advertising, its economics had all gone askew; its editorial touch had become unsure but the idea of a national picture magazine was right and deserves to be revived. Without it, qualities unique to *Life* are missing in American journalism and I think wanted and needed. I promised no laments.

13

SOURCES

To anyone who must deal with the press — in seeking its favor or resisting its curiosity — the experience can be unsettling. A reporter can be helpful to you, or dangerous to you, but whichever the occasion seems to be, it is best to be wary of him.

Early in my police reporting days in Seattle I often visited men or women sitting dejectedly in their cells, not the hangdog losers for whom jail was a familiar experience, but those who had tried to kill themselves or someone else, and now, in a state of grief, shock, remorse or shame, cowered from the reporter. You would tell them that they couldn't escape a story anyway and should seize the chance to get their own version across, and though this was sometimes the case, the offer was fraudulent: I was really after a good story. If asked, I would have said something about the public's right to know; I'm a lot less sure now that the public's morbid curiosity has any such claims, and I have sometimes, while gaining from it, recoiled at the readiness of people to consent so willingly, and volunteer so eagerly, in a destructive invasion of their own privacy. Nowadays one sees people conditioned by watching movies or television to believe that when misfortune occurs it is as much their duty to confide to the camera and to the reporter as to answer a policeman's questions.

In Seattle, I soon graduated to interviewing visiting celebrities, which was less grim than police reporting and easier as well, since they usually wanted attention called to a forthcoming concert or newly published book. Had the exchange been merely a plug, it would have been of little use to either of us, the kind of story that George Axelrod calls interviews-in-shallow. In those brief hotel-room visits I discovered how skillfully celebrities armor themselves against revelation. They knew they must be agreeable but had heard all the questions before, and were not about to lay bare their emotions or get into musical discussions with a reporter who might confuse a caesura with a surgical operation. I suspect that touring opera singers and concert pianists deliberately develop exotic hobbies — raising orchids or collecting antique cars — to satisfy, while diverting, their questioners. An interviewer works to pierce through these convenient little spitballs of organized memory, these neat anecdotes of the practiced subject. Interviews can be a satisfying test of wits. They are duels, which can be a bracing exercise for both parties. Only sometimes does someone get hurt.

To Catch a Personality

Reporters come in all varieties — those who patiently and accurately gather details, whose specialty is information;

those who investigate and prod and harry, whose specialty is disclosure; and those whose specialty is portraiture, either as quick-study artists in one brief interview or as fashioners of full-length profiles.

Interviewing, of the kind that sets out to tell you what a person is like, is of all the branches of journalism the domain of those who are themselves often people of out-sized personality and high ego needs. Some have only elementary scruples: a public figure learns not to be carried away by exchanges of candor with such an interviewer, who will later report his subject's frankness but not his own.

Few people who live by attention — the actress, the politician, the public figure — can afford the haughty obstinacy of the English poet A. E. Housman, who once rejected an interviewer's request: "Tell him that the wish to include a glimpse of my personality in a literary article is low, unworthy and American." For they must always be at the mercy of an interviewer who has the last word, and who if he returns to his typewriter resentful or dis-pleased can shape his article to indicate it. Determined to be interesting even if the person he interviews declines to be, the interviewer often seems to be offering a bargain: "Come on, either give me some indiscreet truth about your-self, or I'll mock you in print."

Nowhere is the process pursued with more cynicism on both sides than in show business. Skilled interviewers can make a man's thought more interesting than it is, and Cary Grant once admitted, "I improve on misquotation." In Hollywood's golden venal years, when gossip columnists could make or break reputations, interviews ran either to scandal or to sycophantic palaver. The new brutal honesty in the journalism of entertainment is hardly progress. An interviewer still has the problem of satisfying the curiosity of fans about some starlet who may only be a teen-ager with an unformed mind, an uncomplicatedly narcissistic temperament and good cheek bones. Worse yet, she may have acquired political opinions of an ardent naïveté. Unwilling to romanticize her, the modern interviewer finds her interesting only to the degree she is candid about her sleeping arrangements. Even more demeaning is the desperate collaboration of fading actresses with interviewers they are right to mistrust.

Such travesties give a bad name to one of modern journalism's glories. When all the bad bargains are acknowledged — the misquoting or misrepresenting, the spiteful or slovenly interviewers with unmerited reputations — I think it must be said that the best of interviews, in their observing and characterizing, as well as in their quoting, often catch the quality of a person in a way he himself could not in speaking for himself. The special art form of the profile has thus gradually replaced the short story in magazines, in much the same way as the camera edged out realistic painting. Both have proved superior witnesses to actuality.

The best interviews are in a sense betrayals, often knowingly entered into by both sides, for as André Malraux remarked, "The truth about a man lies first and foremost in what he hides." Once satisfied that an interviewer is not trying to catch out a subject but just seeking to discover his truths, people often cooperate with their interviewers out of a fascination with how their own character is being revealed (as John P. Marquand was later to fashion a novel from the experience of finding himself and his friends exhaustively interviewed for a *Time* cover story on him).

Even when listening to someone he admires, an interviewer has his ear always cocked for a telling phrase, a remark that is a giveaway of character. The talented interviewers I knew at *Life* were not content to define character in catchphrases out of Freud; they knew people to be most fascinating in their contraries, and might spend weeks trying to reduce the complexity of a person's character into a five-thousand-word article. Watching them, I came to worry less about a complaint sometimes voiced by contemporary historians.

They fear that future biographers will have trouble documenting the private thoughts of today's public figures, who travel a great deal, communicate only in letters that are terse, hurried and businesslike, decide most matters over the telephone, and leave behind no leisurely telltale correspondence in which to discover their motives. I think that future historians will discover that perceptive journalists, getting there first, have asked many of the questions whose answers history will want to hear. I suspect that earlier public figures, seen only through their thoughtful letters and formal speeches, were able to arrange a more reassuring picture of themselves. Modern interviewers refuse to make a flattering official portrait, needing your weaknesses for contrast, and will not pose you so that your weak chin is hidden. The result is a lively and living likeness. I suspect that future historians will be grateful.

Secondary Ignorance

The relationship between reporter and source is at its most benign when a reporter must educate himself in order to pass the knowledge along. In this role, he is appreciative brain-picker. At *Time* magazine we had frequent cause to admire the readiness of scientists, doctors and economists to explain complicated matters in laymen's terms. Some, whom Saul Bellow calls "the publicity intellectuals," are eager to trade an epigram for a mention. But most specialists give of their time believing that matters they know about should be understood correctly by the public. Scientists and specialists no longer avoid reporters, as they once did, in the belief that anything written about their field would be wrong, superficial or sensationalized. Journalism has raised a generation of reporters quite at home in difficult fields, and properly mindful of Einstein's dictum that "everything must be made as simple as possible, but not one bit simpler."

Yet for all the self-educating of reporters, and the emergence each year of hundreds of thousands of Americans schooled in special disciplines, journalism falls steadily behind in reporting the accretion and complexity of scientific knowledge. Perhaps this has as much to do with the public's capacity to comprehend as with the journalist's ability to translate the abstruse.

To a scientist, specialization is both inescapable and limiting. Where once Renaissance man cockily took all knowledge as his province, an educated man today can at best know one discipline well, have some useful intuitions about neighboring subjects and only scattering familiarity with others. Of course there also exist generalists, a title which gives academic status to vague accomplishments. If journalists are sometimes classed as generalists, I think of them at best as generalists of the second class. For journalism that appeals to a broad readership deals primarily with secondary ignorance — ignorance of that which is already known. It has little to do with, and little comprehension of, primary ignorance, that is, those labors of creative scientists, artists and philosophers at the frontiers of discovery in their fields. Or as a colleague of mine used to caution us, we don't really report what is going on at the edge of each probing finger of science; our knowledge begins where that finger joins the hand.

The Public's Business

Not until the subject is public affairs does a certain hardening set in between reporter and his news source. Then the public interest adds an edge and a boldness to the journalist's curiosity.

A reporter believes it his duty to subject officials, businessmen, cops and suspects to intensive questioning and if they — particularly officials skilled in glib evasion — are indiscreet, they must pay for it. Publicity is one consequence of misbehavior, and reporters feel no compunction — in fact they feel a moral responsibility — in spreading the word. As the famous nineteenth-century editor A. L. Godkin of the New York *Sun* said to a lady who accused him of scandal-mongering: "The *Sun* cannot be blamed for reporting what God has permitted to happen." This is journalism's celebrated defense, though I have always found it a bit sanctimonious.

Only in small matters will a journalist withhold whatever he believes to be publishable, and he is thus an awkward fellow to have around. He may have to make an enemy when he would prefer to keep a friend. He believes intuitively that suppression of news is bad for society, even when what is reported may be said to be harmful to reputations, embarrassing to a government, damaging to a nation. In wartime, journalism accepts censorship of battle plans and troop movements, but otherwise resists efforts to prevent awkward truths from becoming known. At White House request the New York *Times* in 1962 patriotically withheld what it knew about the impending invasion of Cuba, and later concluded that in doing so it had not in fact served the national interest — for as the Kennedy entourage afterwards acknowledged, advance publicity might have halted the ill-conceived Bay of Pigs. I recall when, just as *Time* was going to press, one of our correspondents in Florida alerted us that the presumed shooting down of an American plane by Castro's men was a phoney, staged episode. But having been tipped off in confidence by Bobby Kennedy of the imminent invasion of Cuba, and having sworn not to mention it in advance, we decided not to print the plane incident either, certain that by the time readers got their magazines they would be much more engrossed in the front page developments of what became the Bay of Pigs. A few days later Adlai Stevenson, not having been told by the Kennedys, waved the fake picture at the United Nations and overnight lost much of his credibility with fellow diplomats. A few such experiences teach journalists that suppression of news, presumably in the national interest, is a dubious business.

There are journalists who wear their antagonism to government officials and politicians as a badge of their honesty. More often source and journalist preserve a careful amiability, professionals each with his job to do. Some journalists, in Washington as at city hall, have over the years by their discretion and knowledge built up the kind of trust that opens doors for them, and must guard against shading the truth for men they like or admire. Not only in sports, but most flagrantly there, do journalists become "a member of the team" and devolop a malady I call Locker Room Reentry. To preserve their easy berths, many sportswriters raise no awkward questions of owners or players, collaborate in arranged falsities and bowdlerized interviews, and thus assume themselves a future locker-room welcome. The Kennedys were surrounded by a claque of such journalists: if you were covering Bobby Kennedy on campaign tour and insisted on your independence, you would wind up in a motel alone at night, filing your story. If you were "trusted" by the Kennedys you would be included in their free-spoken after-hours presence. On *Life* we once accepted such a Kennedy arrangement and gained by the intimate details, but I was uncomfortable about it; what we printed might be true enough, but I was never convinced that it was the sufficient truth.

A more justifiable kind of collaboration with sources is commonplace in Washington, where the real truths of policy or diplomacy are rarely proclaimed formally, and where sources, if asked to go on record, are practiced at lapsing into hearty ambiguities, impenetrable cant or "no comments." Out of this situation comes the irritating but necessary half-world of off-the-record briefings, which cannot be mentioned in print; or background sessions which may only be attributed to official or highly placed sources.

Only in such ways can reporters pick up essential flavor and private explanations of policy. (Leaks are another matter, to be discussed later.) Dependence in this way upon anonymous authority leads easily to abuse, and when "reliable sources" are cited by the best journalists, the laziest and least scrupulous of journalists can take refuge in the same device, repeating as authoritative the ignorant speculations of some junior down the hall. Collaborations in subterfuge can damage either party. No journalist likes putting his own reputation at the service of those who will not stand publicly behind what they privately said. When a trial balloon proves awkward to its launcher and is denied, the public is left unfairly to judge, according to its own prejudices, whether the journalist or the source is lying. An official too may be hurt by excessive candor. Having confided too freely to reporters he trusts, he often finds his remarks turning up in the stories of reporters not similarly pledged to confidence.

One way to get around the difficulties of anonymous sources is the practice of not-for-attribution interviews. Reporters often accept interviews on this basis, then labor to get the most significant points put on record by a bargaining process that is a form of corrected spontaneity. The source is able to speak freely to a journalist and himself decide, at the end of the interview or later, which of his remarks may be directly quoted. This may seem like connivance to those who think of all journalism as arm's-length entrapment or to those who act as if every press conference should be turned into a show trial or a bear-baiting act. I think it is always journalism's duty to seek clear explanations from sources who may not wish to be frank and forthcoming. But I've never thought the object was to harass a man into saying what he didn't intend and didn't mean.

14

PRESIDENTS

Honeymoons with the press never last with any President; they soon turn into quarrelsome marriages. Every President in modern times has left office convinced that press criticism exceeded the bounds of fairness, and has usually left behind some grumpy comments on journalism.

Reporters in Franklin Roosevelt's day were New Dealers in sympathy, but a majority of newspaper owners were so opposed to him, so ready to misrepresent him, that only by radio "fireside chats" and his gift for commanding front page attention was Roosevelt able to get his message across to the public straight. Whatever later could be said of Richard Nixon's dislike of the press, nothing in Nixon's record equals the sheer nastiness of FDR figuratively awarding an opposition reporter a Nazi Iron Cross.

John Kennedy followed eagerly what the press said about

him. Each week a copy of *Time* was specially airlifted from our Chicago printer to the White House (Luce once complained that Kennedy saw his copy of the magazine earlier than Luce did). The President or his wife would sometimes be on the phone Sunday mornings commenting or complaining to John Steele or Hugh Sidey of *Time*'s Washington bureau. Such attention was flattering but unseemly, and the best of Washington correspondents soon found themselves professionally distancing themselves from a man they liked: the pleasure of his company was at the risk of being compromised. Lyndon Johnson could belabor correspondents in private for hours, alternately sweet-talking them or cussing them out. Nixon — though much criticized by reporters for his inaccessibility and the infrequency of his press conferences — was by comparison frugal and correct in the few private interviews he permitted. Perhaps the truth is that he trusted journalists sympathetic to him only marginally more than his journalistic enemies.

The Nixon administration deserves a special unsavory place in the long history of presidential conflict with the press. Coming to office, Nixon proclaimed, in an expression out of his lawyer's training, that he favored an adversary relationship with the press. That at least promised an absence of hypocrisy.

The men around Nixon had a special antipathy for journalists. Like the man they served — having linked their ambitions to his in the long years out of power — they were private, suspicious, hard-nosed and devious. It took Watergate to demonstrate what they meant by an adversary relationship. Walter Hickel, Nixon's secretary of the interior, had found out earlier, in the final interview in which he was fired by the President: "He repeatedly referred to me as an 'adversary.' It was only after the President had used the term many times and with a disapproving inflection that I realized that he considered an adversary an enemy."

Because Nixon's key subordinates came out of lawyering and advertising, his administration became a fatal mix of special pleading, artfully calculated strategies, sloganized explanations of positions endlessly repeated, and systematic manipulation of opinion. Its best policies were rarely honestly proclaimed, and the worst were hidden or lied about. The administration showed an aversion to general debate — inside its own counsels, with members of its own party in Congress, or with the public — it wanted its own version of events accepted as truth, and believed that the public could be made to distrust and discount everything else. It was as if Nixon longed to live in the last days of the Chinese empire, when all teahouses carried this notice: "The acts of those in authority must not be discussed by those who are not in authority." The White House sought to dry up alternate sources of information in government by reprisals against those who talked too freely to journalists ("big mouths mean little careers" was the way this policy got translated at the Pentagon). Reporting that the administration could not attack in specific detail it set out to discredit on general terms, led by Spiro Agnew's attack on the eastern "liberal" press establishment. But liberal bias was never at the heart of the conflict; something much more fundamental was: the capacity of the press to get at the news and to report it.

Press "neutrality" of mind was hard to sustain towards an administration which set up a White House "communications" office to complain about Washington reporters to their editors, and to put pressure on the owners of newspapers, magazines and television stations. Magazines were threatened with sharply increased postal rates, public television with withholding of federal funds unless it reduced its coverage of public affairs; the disfavored Washington *Post* found its possession of a profitable Florida television channel challenged.

Uppermost on the administration's mind was the power of television's impact. Nixon himself made more use of the presidential prerogative to command prime time than had any President before him (this presidential advantage badly needs balancing by political opponents, not commentators). Nixon feared television's power in other hands. "It's all over if you get chopped up on the networks," said Patrick Buchanan, Nixon's favorite speech writer. "You never recover. The newspapers can beat hell out of you and you've got no problem." And so the administration proposed an ingenious remedy that played on the cupidity and the conservative political outlook of those who own television's valuable franchises. Their broadcast licenses would be renewed for five years instead of the customary three if they in return would undertake to censor network news themselves; they would be judged by their ability to stop what the Nixon apparatus called, but was never ready to define closely as, "ideological payola" and "elitist gossip."[1] Not much of Nixon's economic threats to the press ever got put into practice; the remedies were perhaps too legally doubtful, but they served as intended to intimidate the timid.

[1] The President himself professed neither to read newspapers nor to watch TV news. In an interview on his sixtieth birthday, he said: "I would go up the wall watching TV commentators. I don't. I get my news from the news summary the staff prepares every day and it's great; it gives all sides."

This digest, for the eyes of the President and his inner staff alone, was the work of his speech writer Patrick Buchanan. A copy of it fell into a newsman's hands. He found it full of rancorous sarcasm and bizarrely selected quotations. The chief victim of monopolistic, distorted summary of American public opinion, full of "ideological plugola," thus appears to be the President himself.

The evidence is all there in those interchanges of White House memos since made public: John Dean's enemy lists of newsmen, in order to use "the available Federal machinery to screw our political enemies"; Jeb Magruder commenting against the networks that "just a possible threat of antitrust violations would be effective in changing their views" and "just a threat of IRS investigation will probably turn their approach"; Lawrence Higby urging an attack on Chet Huntley even after he had retired as one of NBC's anchormen because "what we are trying to do is to tear down the institution"; H. R. Haldeman giving orders "to pound the magazines and the networks" and to concentrate this on the few places that count, which would be NBC, *Time, Newsweek* and *Life,* the New York *Times* and the Washington *Post.*"[2] (Haldeman's 1970 list is a fairly accurate cataloguing of forceful independent journalism, though CBS and the Los Angeles *Times* have a grievance in being left off.)

Those who saw a menacing pattern in Nixon's open and covert war on newspapers, magazines and television were saved from paranoia by the evidence that similar means were used against other groups the administration was after.

[2] Within hours after *Life* refused to print a tendentious letter from the White House Communicator at full length, I was subjected to a typically penny-ante Nixonian reprisal: a telephone call from the editor of a Republican "newsletter" which existed to expose or to ridicule press critics. He had been "asked" to check a report that *Time* and *Life* were about to move their headquarters from New York to Chicago. Certainly not, I replied; why should we? Well, it had been suggested to him that we felt the need "to get in touch with middle America." I could see the nasty little story he had in mind. We then played a game of geographical advantages: moving to Cedar Rapids, I said, might gain an editor an insight into farm problems but make him less knowledgeable about urban troubles. I asked my caller where he was from; he was from Florida, and conceded when asked that living in Washington, D.C., often made him feel "out of touch" with the rest of the country. In any case, I told him, whenever I put on my jacket in Rockefeller Center and went off to lunch I felt that I was walking among Americans; didn't he think I was? He seemed to lose heart for his squalid assignment; nothing came of it.

Such efforts were made efficient by the loyalty of ambitious men, made dangerous by the policing powers they wielded, and made self-righteous by men who thought little scrupulosity was owed to those who stood in their way.

If Watergate showed that journalism had not invented its darkest suspicions, it did not dispel the notion that the press had its own interest, as indeed it had, in showing up the covert activities of the Nixon administration. For many Americans, journalists were now seen as conscious partisans. And this was a more damaging loss to journalism than any victory it gained in having its version of the Nixon administration, rather than the administration's own self-serving assertions, ultimately accepted as truth by the public.

If there was a case to be made against the press, the Nixon administration was in no moral position to make it. How could it protest leaks, when its own dirty tricks squads were lavishly endowed to shadow political enemies, raid their quarters and tap their phones, to gather discreditable information which could then be leaked to friendly reporters to "portray a negative image" of their opponents? How could it protest press misconduct when it felt entitled to burgle reporters' homes to find where their information came from?

How could the President argue the principle of free-spoken confidentiality within government while himself taping private conversations without the knowledge of those confiding in him, or ordering taps on the telephones of highly trusted men in government?

Still, confidentiality is indeed essential in government to any honest exchange of opinion and advice. I can see no press "right" to know the private counsels of public men, and I recognize that governments are often handicapped, particularly in foreign affairs, when their private bargaining positions, or candid reflections, become public knowledge. A government's desire to preserve its own secrets is at least as proper as the press's insistence on protecting the confidentiality of it sources. But what the press has no "right" to demand to know about government often falls into its hands.

Leaks are an essential, random and troubling ingredient of newsgathering; for editors as for Presidents their timing is uncontrollable, their contents unpredictable. In normal times, leaks are rarely crucial in public affairs. They may bring to light someone's personal indiscretions for a tittle-tattle paragraph in a Washington gossip column or turn up some isolated misfeasance in office. Journalists, when offered such information, usually first ask themselves whether the source hopes to plant a misleading version of the facts. What's he up to? Foreign embassies may leak information to journalists when they feel that what is being privately negotiated puts their country at a disadvantage. Politicians may confide what went on behind closed doors to curry favor with reporters, to embarrass the opposition, or to deter a course. Gordon Strachan, one of those corruptibly ambitious aides cloned by the Nixon administration, once carefully catalogued five varieties of leaks. He thought nothing could be done when men consciously violated confidences out of their own conception of the national interest, but was convinced that if bureaucrats weren't allowed to be too chummy with the press, one could avoid "the self-serving leak which strengthens the individual policy position by acquiring public support before the final decision is made" or "the ego-stroke leak where the individual either wants to see his name in print or to be known as one with influence." Police and government officials exchange useful tips with friendly newsmen and leak to them information that they want made public even though it could not be introduced as evidence in court (the initial source of *Life* magazine's exposure of the Mafia). Lawyers may confide what a client told a grand jury, to get his version of the story into print before an expected indictment. In the competitive world of journalism, there's no way to make journalists agree never to listen to confidences, or agree not to pursue clues. Journalists themselves distinguish sharply between the self-serving motives of those who provide the tips and leaks, and the usefulness of the information that is offered: theirs not to worry if someone gains or loses by the disclosure; what matters is the accuracy and importance of the facts. Does that end their responsibility? Walter Pincus would have their private calculations made public, requiring journalists to indicate in their stories who stands to benefit from what is being disclosed.

In Washington, D.C., where power is the leading industry, information is power. Information is valuable to own, valuable to withhold, valuable to discover. And so a continuing war exists between those who would hide and those who seek. Leaks first began to take on critical importance in the days of Vietnam, that undeclared and unpopular war fought in a secrecy directed not only against the enemy but against the American public. Military men found themselves asked to fight fastidiously against an enemy who wasn't similarly restricted, or else forced to conceal the methods they and their allies were using, and fell into a self-righteous pattern of misleading, concealing and lying. Equally frustrated men who thought the Vietnamese war immoral and endless, pleaded a higher morality in confiding the secrets of the Pentagon papers to journalists, and arrogated to themselves (as did editors) the decision that most of what was stamped secret was in any case of no current military value, whose exposure would only be inconvenient to the government.

The Nixon administration added further to this unhealthy climate by its curiously insecure and secretive behavior in all other matters, so that even after winning an electoral landslide it still behaved like a besieged administration with an uncertain mandate. Of course, as things turned out, it had a great deal to hide. Faced with constant dissembling and deceiving by the White House, the press could only increase its efforts to discover the reality behind a public relations performance that was not to be trusted. But what really brought everything into the open was a growing unease inside government itself at the enormity of the wrongdoing, and the degree to which ruthless men were entrenching themselves in power.

The government bureaucracy's role in the uncovering of Watergate has been insufficiently celebrated. The press has taken most of the credit, as well as the calumny, but a press merely hostile or suspicious of the administration could not have achieved its victories without vital evidence furnished by disillusioned or discontented bureaucrats. James Madison and Alexander Hamilton never foresaw that one of the crucial checks and balances against too powerful an executive branch would be news leaks.

As congressional hearings and public investigators, each with the power of subpoena, dug deeper, as misbehavior became criminal charge, as prosecutors became rivals for public attention and politicians saw new futures for themselves as crusaders, leaks, tips and confidences became a new cottage industry. Much that was leaked shouldn't have been: grand jury proceedings should be secret, private memos ought to be private; accusations of corrupt practices should be settled in the courts. Efforts are under way in a number of states, through agreements reached between judges and editors, to limit pre-trial publicity in ways that do not compromise the independence of the press nor conceal what deserves to be known. Men in public life rightfully complain that it is all but impossible to sue the press successfully under the Supreme Court's ruling in *New York Times* v. *Sullivan,* which allows no redress for printed error about public men so long as it was published without malice. The special fervor and animosity that marked the journalism of the Watergate period came from a gradual awareness of how widespread misfeasance had become, and the evidence that government itself would not scruple to conceal or destroy evidence or pervert justice. In that atmosphere, Agnew and others might complain of being condemned in the press before being tried in the courts. Yet those anonymous sources which the press was criticized for quoting, held up remarkably well later. Readers might fear that undocumented denunciations made it hard for them to be fair in their own minds to the accused, but when it came to specific and grave charges of criminal misconduct, sources which were irritatingly anonymous to the reader had to be known and judged responsible by reporters.

The conviction that a cornered administration was powerful, unprincipled and evasive, also gave a sharper edge to reporters' questions whenever Nixon emerged from hiding for a rare press conference. The press in its individual competitiveness has always felt it improper to gang up on a President with a series of agreed questions and therefore any press conference is uncontrolled and rough-edged, but all the more so when Nixon astutely called on the more abrasive reporters in order to create public sympathy for himself. Even if Nixon had forfeited his own right to be treated with respect, the office he held deserved respect. The decline in press conference manners might be righted in the future by a President who commanded more respect — but possibly not, since one law that never seems to be repealed is Gresham's law. But I know of no screening test for admittance to presidential press conferences that would have avoided such scenes, for some of the rudest questioners were by the jobs they held most entitled to be there.

And so, even in the victory of Watergate, after a moment's savoring of triumph, many journalists I think disliked being cast in the role of relentless antagonists to the President. Supine capitulation to a President, and particularly this one, was of course not possible to the press. By their questions, journalists must follow the biblical injunction to speak truth to power. But in this period a heavier burden was being placed upon the press, as defender of common liberties, than was healthy for it to bear. In Great Britain, the prime minister and his chief ministers each day face a question period in the House of Commons where they undergo scrutiny from opposition members not only about policy but about specific performance. I once thought it a happy accident that the presidential press conference had developed into an American counterpart of this useful procedure. But the crucial difference is that the press lacks the legitimacy of being elected representatives and the understood status of a loyal opposition. During Watergate, when the nation was faced with an arbitrary and highhanded President unwilling to answer forthrightly, and a fractious and irresolute Congress hesitant to call him to account, the press was in effect a bastion of the public interest. Cheers for that: its investigations in time became the proper business of the courts. But its angry cross-examinations of the President were an inquisition without legal status, and its frustrated hectoring of the President came at some cost to the journalistic reputation for independence.

For the press, in its newsgathering as opposed to its

editorializing function, cannot treat even a hostile administration as an enemy and become equally partisan and unfair. Nor can the press aspire to destroy the power of government, for as Tocqueville recognized, "it is both necessary and desirable that the government of a democratic people should be active and powerful; and our object should not be to render it weak or indolent, but solely to prevent it from abusing its aptitude and strength."

Journalism does have to keep unsleeping watch on any administration's more dubious activities, which is good discipline for the presidency. But journalism is also required to report every administration's words fairly, to analyze its actions and acknowledge its achievements, all of which is good discipline for journalists. A lively tension between press and government serves the public good. The process works somewhat in the way that Justice Holmes once wryly described the philosophy of antitrust legislation: you must compete, but no one must win the competition. And when the press seems to win, it is most in danger of losing. For when any President seeks to prove the press its determined enemy, and not to be trusted because of that, his case must not be rendered provable to unprejudiced minds.

15

EDITING

Night-table Thoughts

• Newspaper editors create a new landscape every day, in which the figures may not be related but do have a common place in the scene, some in the foreground, some as part of a distant grouping. Next day the editor comes to work, looks at his live tableau, sees that it now looks a little different, and asks querulously: "Who moved?"

• If you live by words you come to realize how many of them are unneeded. This realization almost, but not quite, reduces you to silence; it does put you in mind of Robert Louis Stevenson: "If I knew how to omit, I would ask of no other knowledge."

• Journalists may not wish to admit that they too are in the business of fashion — which is the skillful commercial exploitation of novelty, satiety and boredom. They resent the taunt of superficiality but are in fact specialists in attention span, in timing, and in the shelf life of ideas.

• Journalism has a success bias, particularly when it comes to politicians, entertainers and athletes. Who wants to read about the worn-out, the overfamiliar, the has-been? Who can bear to watch the aged, overmuscled, tense-faced hoofer with a sad desperate smile, who means to entertain but spreads melancholy instead? The journalism of careers is a parabola in which the down side is not visible until, years later, reading of a death in a nursing home, you say, why I thought he was dead long ago. There's a limit to journalism's commitment to the disagreeable truth: it brings you the winner of the lottery but not the thousands who failed in the draw.

• Editors may think of themselves as dignified headwaiters in a well-run restaurant but more often operate a snack bar, full of desperate saves and scurries, and expect you to be grateful that at least they got the food to the table warm.

• Journalism constructs momentarily arrested equilibriums, and gives disorder an implied order. That is already two steps from reality.

• A man keeping tabs on fifty subjects will have little to add to any of them, except perhaps a sense of their relationships and priorities.

• Journalism arrogantly acknowledges no limits to what it may choose to be curious about, and few limits to its capacity to reckon with it.

- Some things journalists can understand, others for the moment only relate, like Auden's definition of a poem: a clear expression of a mixed feeling. If we cannot provide answers, we must settle for lucid statements of the common confusion.

- The compulsion to run a serious article sets in motion in every editor a desire to counter it with something light as a change of pace. The real world isn't so obliging.

- Journalists react much as stomachs do to what they are given, reclassifying everything matter-of-factly. The taste-buds may respond to cake, steak and caviar. The stomach says that to me it's all just fats, carbohydrates and proteins, and let's hear no more nonsense about it.

- To bring any complex public issue into focus, an editor operates much as does the Speaker in the House of Commons as he assembles an effective debate. The Speaker sees to it that those in power and on the opposition front bench are heard first; then he calls upon those members with known qualifications on the subject as sponsor or expert witness; finally everyone is given a chance to be heard, with known bores and unknown amateurs consigned to the off hours. It may seem an arbitrary power in an editor for him to decide who gets heard and who doesn't, but the decision rarely turns on an editor's own prejudices, more on his practiced conjecture of who will be interested. He has little of the kind of power which is most to be enjoyed, that of being capricious.

- Journalists have to chronicle the foolishness of the time as well as the accepted wisdom, because one sometimes turns out to be the other.

• If busy editors operate with any underlying philosophical premise at all, it is as simple as that of the elderly judge who after a lifetime of listening to conflicting evidence was persuaded — not that all men are liars — but of the many-sidedness of truth.

Judgments and Responsibilities

Over the years, so gradually that at no remembered moment did I become conscious of the shift, I discovered that being an editor changes one's outlook. No longer could I say, as do so many reporters, that they have no truck with the meaning of events, that's for others — the editorial writer perhaps, or the reader himself; they just lay out the facts as they have found them. An editor can hardly plead such innocence of responsibility. In his assignments, in his selection of what others write, he puts together a finished work of transitory interest that inevitably has his own mark upon it.

He may solemnly deny any conscious attempt to find meaning in events. Thus Harold Ross aimed for urbanity in editing *The New Yorker* magazine — politics was ignored, and serious argument was left to the dull-witted. That mood and tone began to seem out of key during the depression; it seemed mannered and frivolous in the anxieties and perils of the Second World War, and was abandoned. Since then, under its second editor, William Shawn, the magazine is no longer afraid to be serious; no longer elegantly detached, it allows itself anger and derision. *The New Yorker* might even own, but for the pomposity of it, to feeling a responsible citizen.

For me, the legacy of Luce, the years of contending with a moralizing man, have left me with an unfashionable compulsion to find pattern and useful direction in events. I know other journalists who think such an attitude presumptuous; for them, in the present complexity of affairs, truths can only be partial and personal. Perhaps; but I think a reader wants more, even if he is searchingly critical of the attempt, as he should be.

How responsibly then does the American press do its job? I think the answer should be confined narrowly to that functional part of journalism which makes of them *news*papers, ignoring those sprawling, broad acres of newsprint devoted to sports, to stock market tables, to recipes and instructions for fixing screendoors — all that apparatus which caters, legitimately but lengthily, to the public interest in leisure, moneymaking, and diversion. With less justice to the press, I propose also to leave aside that important motley which is local news coverage. In many American papers the first question to be asked about their international and national coverage is, where is it? Half a front page, and a few trailing columns inside: wire stories which at full length are informative are often truncated into meaninglessness. Thick American newspapers, which to foreigners seem so squandering of space, often provide thin news diets. No wonder newsmagazines prosper, not simply as digests of the week's news, but often bringing news that many readers can't find in their local newspapers.

The truth is, the more serious the reader the better he is served by American journalism. He who would be well informed cannot be content with a television newscast, nor in all likelihood by his daily newspaper; the more he cares about any subject the more he can gratify his continuing curiosity about it only by tracking it down in a variety of newspapers, newsmagazines, journals of opinion, television talk shows, and books so timely as to be themselves journalistic. I think such a reader — content to take neither

all his information nor his opinions from one source —
is well served in American journalism's prolific variety, and
will find more information available to him than anywhere
else on earth. A reader gets as good a journalism as he is
willing to work at.

Europe's great sober journals, such as *Le Monde* and
Neue Zuricher Zeitung, excel in serious analysis of international affairs; the best of England's newspapers are more
literate than ours, particularly in their cultural coverage,
but the worst, in all their plenty, pander cheaply to the
envy, titillations and resentments of a lower class audience
whom they seem to understand well and to scorn. French
journalism at its finest is intelligent, but rarely disturbs the
corrupt and authoritarian aspects of those who govern
France and rule its society. Only in America is the press so
unhampered in its inquiries, so aggressive in its pursuit, so
fruitful in what it discovers. Its success doesn't mean that
there is more to be uncovered here than anywhere else:
think what six months of enterprising reporting in Moscow
would show of the corruption, incompetence, favoritism
and injustice to be found there!

Perhaps no more than a thousand American journalists
provide most of the crucial reporting of national and international affairs, though many others batten off them. The
press associations and the radio and television networks
have their own men in Washington and in foreign capitals,
but as quickly pass along the enterprise of others, usually
acknowledging their debts, if only to place responsibility for
what is said. (This borrowed quality in news dissemination,
I suspect, provides an unreasoning resentment in those listening to news that displeases them; it becomes doubly offensive to hear it from a news announcer on a local television channel who with resonant voice and unearned air
of knowledgeability reads what he had no part in gathering.)

The news itself originates in a small body of men, and there is sometimes a pack quality about their interests and their judgments. In the recent disorder of the times, they have had to report much that goes against the popular grain — to describe, despite official claims to the contrary, a war that was not being won, to a nation used to victory; to report of an administration which had suited itself carefully to the public mood, that such an administration was in fact unworthy of trust.

Coverage that begins as a lone outrage that the truth should be concealed soon turns into something far different when the entire press corps takes it up, scenting public interest. The effect can be like those crime waves that tabloid newspapers used to detect, though the evidence was not to be found in the statistics. Soon the story takes on artificial momentum. Once a theme to the news emerges — that McGovern vacillates, that Lyndon Johnson has a credibility problem, that Nixon has much to hide — then any small fact, otherwise inconsequential, can be tied to the theme and made to seem news. No wonder the victim thinks he is being persecuted. This tendency was present in Watergate — but so was a journalistic intuition that many avenues waited to be explored, and some if followed down would open wider. That instinct was right.

If you ask me whether the lacks, the biases, the blunders or the excesses to be found in press coverage are fatal to its reliability, I answer, not if you read journalism skeptically. If you say the news is often too much for you, I sympathize. If you say you can't believe anything you read in the papers or hear on television, I ask you to name your better sources.

16

FUTURES

Once I thought of journalists as disturbers of the peace. Perhaps many people still do. Journalists won't leave well enough alone, and seem to be always belittling, always puncturing. This negativism, so often evident in manner, is like a CPA's impatience with facile explanations from his client ("just give me the exact figures") in his efficient pursuit of a true account. I have since come to believe that journalism, though required to be skeptical and often thought to be destructive, is in a final sense an affirming occupation. It forever seeks to construct an implied equilibrium out of chaos; to state how things stand at the moment, so that they can be acted upon. This positive conviction that the world can be made sense of — and that only by seeing things straight will the right decisions be made — may be the ultimate distortion of reality the press is guilty of, for the momentary equilibriums that we make may not be the ones that history assigns to our times.

These equilibriums exist rather formlessly in the back of an editor's mind, determining how he plays stories; he hesitates to define the equilibrium too clearly for fear that doing so would dominate his reactions and blind him to contrary evidence. Don't look to him for assured apocalyptic views, or for that final tightening of argumentation that dismisses alternate possibilities: his line of work requires of him a zone of tolerance that is wider than that which comes naturally to partisans or visionaries.

He is also required to take into account the public's sense of its own situation, and here he moves beyond the assured world of facts into imponderables. An editor's intuition about the public mood determines at any moment how much of a hearing he gives to the soothers, how much to the indignant.

Future Despair

In recent years, America's quarrel with itself has been so deep that anyone must wonder whether the natural American sense of optimism about its future is recoverable. Will we ever speak so casually of ourselves again as "we the people"? Will we feel again what Ernest Renan meant by a nation: "to have common glories in the past, a common wish in the present; to have done great things together, to wish to do greater; these are the essential conditions that make up a people."

The question of the nation's confidence in itself is constantly in an editor's mind, and when he suspects (as I do) a gap between a public's reading of its own situation and what he thinks it to be, he gets busy seeking the evidence to test or reject his own thesis. Whether America's future can be democratically controlled, and for good ends, I believe to be one of the great journalistic subjects of the 1970s. I propose to examine it in this final chapter, and even to lay down a bet on it; not in order to promote a false heartiness about our condition, but because I believe that the prevailing public mood — an anarchy of separate despairs — misreads the potentialities.

The French philosopher Saint-Simon divided history into alternating periods that he called the organic and the critical. In organic periods some positive creed animates all actions, and people under its influence go as far as they can with it, and finally outgrow it. Then comes a period of criticism and negation in which the only prevailing conviction is that all the old convictions are false. John Stuart Mill thought he lived in such a transitory period when "the old opinions in religion, morals and politics are so much discredited in the more intellectual minds as to have lost the greater part of their efficacy for good, while they still have life enough in them to be a powerful obstacle to the growing of any better opinion on these subjects."

We too live in the drafts and angry winds of a transition. The most stylish advice we get is that of René Dubos: "In a changing world, it is more important to be adaptable than to be perfectly adapted." Presumably Dubos does not merely mean that we should become as adaptable as the tumbleweed, which drifts where it is blown, for that would be a counsel of helplessness.

Despair of the future has settled over those Americans who are usually the most congenitally optimistic — those hearty, hard-working Americans who believe in effort as the solvent for all difficulty. For such positive thinkers, the world seems lately to have spun out of assured orbit; change is no longer the bracing challenge it once seemed to be, but a fearsome overlapping series of menaces that they have lost the ability to control.

The extremer version of this mood is the siege mentality, which can conceive of an acceptable future for itself only by multiplying the apparatus of mistrust — abroad more missiles, bigger navies and truculent diplomacy; at home more laws, more locks, gates, safes, vaults, watchmen, inspectors, policemen, judges, guards, fences, barricades. Stabilized inequality is what many people mean by law and order. The philosophical expression of their fears was heard in Nixonian calls for new rigor against the perils of permissiveness; when he was not defending his own conduct but attacking the conduct of others, he worried whether the United States had entered a Roman decline. (Personally I believe that historical parallels make sloppy arguments, and agree with the English historian A. J. P. Taylor that the present helps one to understand the past and not the other way around.)

Oddly, a similar despair about the future haunts the speech and action of those most eager for change. The dominant literary mode of our time is a mordant hopelessness. The cinematic hero of an age which has no heroes is the copout and the dropout, without roots or purpose, the easy rider who is either wry or self-pitying, whose brutality or crudity or self-destructiveness is not be be charged against him but is presumably explicable in the awfulness of our times.

That such pessimism should simultaneously govern both those who long to restore America's traditional vision of itself, and those most eager to reject it, suggests a common fear of the future that comes, I believe, from the velocity of change. Few in America any more seem to consider the future a friend.

Perhaps this is because our vision of it arrives either in the antiseptic white of science fiction movies — cardboard people in plastic spacecraft — or in the numbing projections we hear from the statisticians. Computerized projections, with their air of inevitability, are brandished over us like machetes. Even those who live by hunch and common sense must keep a grudging eye on them. Extrapolations from present trends do indeed warn early of exhaustible resources and spur a search for alternatives. But just beyond this useful knowledge lies the fantasy playground of the futurologists. They dazzle with their intersecting trend lines, but in their little noticed footnotes caution that the predictions they make are "surprise free," that is, they exclude in their projections what is most certain about the future, its unforeseeable surprises. For them to reckon in the ability of a society to correct course would be unscientific. Human unpredictability must also be disregarded, since numbers cannot be assigned to it. Such fascination with bloodless data, I think, has already done much to hasten the collapse of political liberalism in the United States. An academic elite, liberal in intentions, came to believe that politics is only the art of problem-solving; if you assemble the right data, people would choose the right alternatives. From this point of view, ideology was unnecessary, and politics the vulgar art of the self-serving. Before problems could harden into issues, the new tools of statistics and forecasting would have "identified" and dealt with them. In this way, Appalachia was discovered not by its own outcries (which conventional politics used to respond to, seeking votes as well as solutions) but on charts of deprivation.

Planning has won its victory, and the battles are now over specifics, not philosophy. I quarrel only when planners, made intolerant by their monopoly of data, declare their own formula for change inescapable (like it or not) and indivisible. To me, change is more like the traffic on the roads of India. The best driver I ever knew was a Sikh, trained in the British army, who could make great modulations of speed without his passengers being aware of any abrupt change. His swift progress down crowded two lane Indian roads was achieved not merely by calculating, as on an American expressway, the actions of other drivers traveling more or less at the same speed. Instead he had a virtuoso's quick perception of the likely responses of others on the road who were traveling in two directions and at four levels of speed — of cars hurtling down the road as fast as he was; of cyclists weaving in and out; of slowly moving carts drawn by bullocks; of streams of people walking, or stopping suddenly to talk. To me, changing America is more like that Indian road — a confusion of movements at varying speeds — than like the uniform, onrushing movement of an American superhighway.

A Parity of Impediments

In America's headlong rush to the future, the pace has previously been determined by business. When corporations or individuals are singlemindedly engaged in increasing their own wealth, they can move quickly, while decisions in a democracy that require a common consent are beset by delays and lassitude. This advantage of private initiative was once considered natural right: wasn't that how the West was won? Any challenge to the right of industry to seek its own self-interest required a showing of grievous injustices. During the depression, smokestacks meant jobs, and what more needed to be said?

A new public philosophy more suited to affluence has

taken hold. Many signs of a changed attitude seem temporary in their faddishness, but should instead be seen, I believe, as successive examples of more lasting change. The social contract between business and society is being rewritten. Business no longer has a blank check. An irritated public is coming to demand that those who pollute shall bear the cost of its cleaning up; those who destroy the amenities of others with their highways or airports or factories have obligations to those they distress. But the brief against business does not stop here. Its compulsion to getting ever bigger has not, as promised, brought about better and cheaper products, or in many cases even better management. The biggest corporations, whether in automobiles or electronics, have serious problems in quality control of their products. Mergers and conglomerates do much to destroy employee feelings of intimacy and participation; if executives complain of a lack of "loyalty up" there is frequently little loyalty down. The affection that employees once felt for their firms, and the faith that customers felt in products, now seem an advertiser's hustle: the relationships are less sentimental and less grounded in awe. Now shoddy products and slippery sales techniques must answer to the organized outcries of consumerism.

And so, even administrations that come to power heavily financed by business, and indebted to it, find themselves imposing on manufacturers new standards of purity and reliability, and on sellers demands that they merchandise their products honestly. Businessmen characteristically oppose most of the changes that will make their endeavors more respected again. I believe that Americans have only begun to use the levers of public incentive to prohibit or encourage behavior, a trend that will make industry and business, like government, more subject to the frustrating process of obtaining multiple public consents. The immediate result may only be to multiply lawyers and lobby-ists. But the process should also lead to some parity in impediments, making change more manageable.

The Flaw in the American Dream

In the contemporary American mood, uncertainty about the future is matched by a restless dissatisfaction with the present. Affluence has produced a discontent that was not anticipated in the single-minded pursuit of it. Where fear of joblessness is no longer the arbiter of performance on any job, the result is sloth and carelessness of workmanship, and indifference or discourtesy in service.[1] And, as the many get what only the few once enjoyed, so much else changes. With products that can be efficiently multiplied, affluence permits efficient distribution. But whenever service is mass-produced, as everyone has come to know, its quality declines. It is not so much the vulgarity of new classes of people who can afford to travel that changes the quality of traveling; it is that they are so many. And this is the flaw that affluence discovers in the American dream.

For though politics proclaims its belief in equality, Americans sort themselves out as a people by economic inequality, which determines how and where they live.[2] The only in-

[1] The word *waiter* now more often defines the served rather than the server. In a widely based prosperity, not only does servility disappear but so does deference; we are lucky to get amiability. A society that puts such emphasis on unequal awards finds it harder to spur a pride in craft among those who are least rewarded.

[2] The exception, of course, is the black. Until he can choose where he lives as a right, not a favor, no one can know how many blacks will want to be randomly dispersed in the population at large, or how many — like other identifiable ethnic groups — will prefer the company, the neighbor-hoods, the habits, the traditions of their own kind. But if America is to honor its sacred political texts, the day has to come when the decision is theirs.

equality that Americans feel at home with is economic: the rest is considered snobbery. Money separates them in good restaurants or lunch counters, in gallery seats or orchestra, in luxury hotels or dumps, in first class or tourist. A friend of mine once declared his belief in "dollar democracy," that is, his money was as good as another's. What he really believed in was money as the unequalizer: the biggest tipper gets the best table. The system works socially because no one is confined to his own category, not permanently, not even temporarily: anytime he wishes, he can blow it all and go first class. A German socialist was once reproached for riding in a first class railway carriage, and replied that he was working for the day when *everyone* would ride first class. It is this that has proved the impossible dream: when all is called first class, nothing is.

From this discovery comes much of the middle class frustration that affluence has not lived up to its promise. Advantage no longer confers its pleasurable individual attention. Scarcities of resources and energy develop; so do a lack of solitude, spaciousness and privacy as the affluent many travel, buy, and spread themselves out.

On the American campuses in the sixties, where almost half of a generation had entered college in the mass pursuit of unequal status, disillusionment with privileged manyness first began. The currency of academic credentials became deflated, the measurable distinction conferred by going to college declined, yet who could quarrel with the democratic notion that everyone should be educated up to the limits of his capacity? For those who under such easy conditions did not get to college, the burden on pride became heavier. I think that the years ahead in the United States will be marked less by rivalries between economic classes than between those with differing amounts of schooling, grouped by the kind of work they do. Their incomes may be relatively equal, between intellectuals with moderate salaries and workers with high wages, but their values will sharply differ. I do not think that journalism has found a way to discuss the incomprehension and tension between these two groups without stereotypes that perpetuate the separation. ("Hardhat" is a typical journalistic label — useful as a metaphor of truculence while disregarding other qualities of the group, or of individuals within it.) I suspect that many college educated people regret an isolation from a public they have left behind and do not understand. College both educates taste and specializes interest and knowledge; both characteristics tend to narrow friendships to those with similar bents, and relationships with others come awkwardly. When this in turn leads to intellectual condescension, however, it is a forbidding and all but incurable trait, and ignores how many people there are who solidly occupy their own spaces, as carpenters and fishermen and farmers often do, and do not ask to be judged by what they are not.[3] I don't believe in romanticizing "ordinary people" as Hollywood used to do, yet I also know how many people preoccupied with living their own lives with a decent regard for family and neighbors are mere statistics on someone else's charts of selfish indifference.

If two sets of values are in contention in this country, I would bet on that community of outlook which has persisted in a generation since the campus revolted, and is to be found as often among those who in that generation did not get to college. I take the core of this attitude to be an acceptance of constriction, a belief that the old faith in progress through the unlimited expansion of individual egos is no longer possible, or if possible, undesirable. Along

[3] I confess here to speaking in the shorthand language of Group — that fatal lumping of people which journalists deplore in demagogues, partisans and ignorant people, but sometimes find an irresistible convenience.

with this goes a rejection of some of the dog-eat-dog mentality that once governed ambition, a readiness to accept technology but not to be enslaved by it, a receptivity to notions such as public control of land use that once seemed socialistic. This attitude in a new generation seems to me more in accord with our evolving future than does the defensive stalwartism of those whom John Maynard Keynes called the elder parrots. The new attitude may be surer in what it refuses than in what it esteems; it lacks exhilaration; its ideas still await successful political articulation, but its impact is going to be felt.

A good life for all — at least for myself — might be said to be its ambition, to be measured less in accumulation of goods than in accumulation of experience (being less materialistic does not require being less selfish). In morals, the accompanying attitude is that the right to one's own pleasures is not for others to question. This is not a formula for a future that will beguile everyone. Nor am I sure that the values (or the "value free" assumptions) of a technologically sophisticated elite, freed from what it sees as the tyranny of creeds, will prove any more inspiriting than did the strivers' mentality of merchants and manufacturers. A democracy free to will its own satisfactions, undeterred by any commanding authority outside itself, suggests a spiritual bleakness.

I am not sure that organized religion will ever regain its central hold, but will exercise sway only on those who come voluntarily to it, which may be no bad thing — already among its own followers the church finds religion experienced rather than dogma obeyed to be a healthier bond. For much of society, then, moral authority has lost the compulsion of necessity. Institutions are suspect and hierarchy resented. The country only reluctantly accepts the power of stabilizing elites: they have been challenged for their misdeeds, their insensitivity, their inadequacy. Many of these institutions — the churches, the schools, corporations — are in the process of reexamining and renewing themselves, but remain under suspicious scrutiny.

Democracy is thus asked to prove itself at a time when its institutions are not in secure command, and when affluence has succeeded in removing economic necessity — true necessity, not merely the satisfaction of wants — from a large part of society. The presence of necessity in those who are "disadvantaged" — the blacks, the poor, the hustling immigrant children — often makes them paradoxically the more advantaged. They seem surer of their direction than so many Americans they move among, who chase only increments in their comfort, and do so in jobs they find uncompelling.

An absence of such necessity, I think, accounted for much of the unreality of campus activism — accounted first for its heightened passion, its impatience with restrictions, and in the end for its swift collapse. For many that emotional experience produced a withdrawal into personal pursuits, a scorn of civic enthusiasm, succeeded by a grudging willingness to "work within the system" without hoping to change it. Civic rejection thus immobilizes great numbers of those who are best equipped to accomplish change in society. But I do not, like futurologists stretching out their trendlines to the horizon, assume this condition to be permanent. The present disillusionment, which is deep seated, is a natural, necessary condition for a turn around. Disillusion, and anguish about what has gone wrong, is a healthier state than despair, and I think more nearly defines the American condition in the mid-1970s. The contemporary impotence is of strengths insufficiently used.

Through education, through travel, through television and films, Americans have become anthologies of many

196

cultures, and less willing to view their own with self-satisfaction. I think it will be some time before the United States finds itself giving moral instruction to the rest of the world. For many Europeans, recent American experience serves more as a warning signal than as the beacon it once was. In part this is because other nations have caught up economically, and find less to envy the United States and their political tasks seem more manageable in the smaller, more settled monocultural societies of Western Europe. The task that America now confronts is also harder than its constitutional forefathers intended, since they did not anticipate a universal electorate when they wrote their noble phrases about equality (they were mindful of the unruly passions of the mass, but did not expect it to have the vote). Americans have the further burden, peculiar to themselves, of including in their plebiscites the wishes and ambitions and counter-tugs of so many minorities, including the ten percent of Americans who are black. Is any other nation further along in giving opportunity to minorities in its midst that once were held down and held back? Hardly two decades separate Negroes sent to the back of the bus, and black mayors in Los Angeles, Atlanta and Detroit.

I suspect my own optimism about America would seem of a wan kind to a confident patriot of Henry R. Luce's generation. But then, the nation has come so close to social disintegration, has suffered such shocks of assassination, has been subjected to such political misrule. I confess that I ask and expect less of democracy than I once did. I don't know that a democracy as big as ours can ever achieve those flowerings of civilization that a past concentration of wealth, leisure and informed tastes — as well as a disregard of the well-being of the lower ends of society — once made possible in privileged pockets of culture in Europe and Asia. Democracy has less to do with the highest standards than with a more equal distribution of well-being and with assuring liberties that are universally shared. In that free space, the rest is up to individuals. Democracy cannot create high art, for example, and is apt to be resistant or indifferent to it. But then creativity works mysteriously within individuals. Their best work is often wrought in opposition to majorities — and yet the highest periods of creativity in history have often accompanied great bursts of economic energy. Foreigners may deplore American politics but often find its arts exhilarating.

The signs that under all its handicaps the United States will be able to respond sensibly to its problems are not yet susceptible to proof, but that assumption affects the way as an editor I respond to news as it happens. I find evidence for such optimism in the way that the public, at turbulent moments, has refused to push matters to their ultimate ends, and this conservative response has by no means been confined to those whose politics are conservative. Against this assumption is the woeful litany of a thousand television talk shows that presume a society winding down: the spread of drugs and crime, the intractability of race, the low moral standards of public and private life, the mass exploitation of greed and envy, the cynicism that "everybody does it and gets away with it." It's not yet safe for Pollyanna to play in the streets.

But I think that any editor, keeping his eye on the atmospheric barometer of public hope or despair, must not only be aware of what is actual but also of a latent potential. And I think there is in this country, at a level deeper than the tawdry political debates which falsely personify the struggle and distort the issues, an emerging national longing to act in community for common ends, because the country has to. It is too soon to rehabilitate the word consensus. But I think profound disagreements in outlook or sense of urgency can be contained again within the norms of civility and politics. This permits a return to that balancing of interests and accepted constraints by which issues, even momentous ones, are traditionally decided or lived with.

For journalism to ignore the evidence of such a mood would be to delay its occurrence. What journalism looks for, in ways that journalists hesitate to admit, has much to do with what they find.

Alternatives — Apocalyptic or Affirmative

Is such a prospect too hopeful? A more apocalyptic judgment on our society issues regularly from our leading novelists, who compete with journalists in trying to define the times both live in, and in recent years have been driven to frenzy or satirical excess to make their fiction more interesting than real life.

The best of novelists excel over journalists in capturing the spirit and random texture of our times, but the respect owed to their eloquent statements of the human predicament is not equally owed to entertainers who play to a taste for the fashionably deprecatory. The difference between a novelist's truths and a journalist's has become blurred. Nowadays novelists double as journalists, wear the same livery and turn up at the same events, and if their presence is sometimes enlivening, it also adds to the confusion: we have factual novels and fictionalized journalism. The line that separates them needs to be more clearly drawn.

Whether a novelist is serious in his labors, or merely shrewd in anticipating market tastes, he is not in his fiction answerable to reality, only to plausibility. He is at every moment free to heighten his effects, and the wild journeys of a novelist's lawless imagination often makes a journalist's reined-in flights of fancy seem like a lumbering ride on a winged percheron. A novelist may tear society apart to illustrate the horror of his vision and feels no need to reassemble it; too much moral imperative would flaw his work. He is society's outsider, painting if he wishes a finished, coherent and unsparing picture of it. That is his valuable contribution to a society he may despise, and he owes it no more.

A journalist cannot, like the novelist, secede from the community. His judgments on society may be severe but are never final: his narrative is always ongoing and untidy; for him there is always more to be discovered and more to be said. He is finally responsible neither to his imagination nor to his sympathies but to the facts. The weight he gives to other people's ideas has less to do with their novelty or worth than with their likely impact on the direction of society. The weight he gives to his own ideas is similarly conditioned by whether they can be sustained by the facts. I believe the task of journalism to be two-fold: to report on its times, and to attempt some understanding of them. The second task is the more critical, and the more easily criticized. But you can't have one without the other; otherwise journalism has done but half its job, and its report is but chaotic fragments meaninglessly assembled.

Few people — other than novelists — would think the press insufficiently apocalyptic. Popular criticism all runs the other way: that journalism is destructive and accents the bad out of cynicism, prejudice or desire for sensationalism. Journalism troubles the respectable; it particularly offends that most formidable caste of respectables, businessmen. They've never had much respect for journalism. In the old days they didn't think they owed anybody explanations for what they did, and held any probing newsman in contempt; if he was too pesky they could always get to the paper's owner, who was a member of the same club as themselves. They hired publicity men to put out favorable stories and to fend off rude queries: at first these were ex-newsmen, paid more money; but later they were advertising men who like Nixon's press agent, Ron Ziegler, were uncontaminated by any previous history of impartial search for the truth.

In time the better corporations developed elaborate publicity departments to tell their own story their way: their in-house magazines, like their stockholders' reports, are well-researched, well-illustrated, lavishly produced. But they are always a *seller's* truth: correct in what they say, but unless required by law, as in SEC disclosure regulations, leaving out unpleasant truths. Businessmen, along with President Nixon, come to think that this cozy way is best for everybody because it is most convenient for themselves. Why can't everyone be so affirmative?

They forget that other side of their own operations which is *buyer's* truth. When these same businessmen want to buy from another, they skip all the apparatus of salestalk, they don't want partial truths and exhortations about the seller's fine qualities, they want to know what they are getting; they want hard knowledge about materials and design, prices, delivery dates and standards. I think journalism is in the business of *buyer's* truth. Never mind whether the result is favorable or unfavorable, negative or positive, let the facts be clearly seen.

The journalist, though a member of the society he monitors, is not an officer of the court. He helps to shape that society, and should endure scrutiny as much as that which he himself scrutinizes. If in the end he is without friends or allies, I think he has no right to feel sorry for his lonely isolation. That independence is what enables him to do his job. He can't, without jeopardizing his work, expect affection. He may think he's entitled to more respect, but longing for it has risks too. At the most he can only hope for, and insist on, some understanding of what he is about.